FIND YOUR AWESOME

Acclaimed Coin Dealer Reveals 10 Secrets to Unleash the Real You

DANIEL RATNER

Table Of Contents

Introduction

In the summer of 1982 while working as a bank teller, four gunmen walked into my branch with their guns waving, screaming for all the customers to get down. I immediately put my hands up.

One of them pointed his gun straight at me and said: "Drop your hands or I'll blow your head off."

In a split second, my life could have ended. I felt like I was going to wet my pants. Dropping my hands wasn't a hard decision to make.

It was a harrowing experience, but as with the emotional after effects of any traumatic event, you can control *them* or they can control *you.* We have no power over when our lives will end, but we can master our emotions and how we feel and think about ourselves.

In this book, I hope to help you realize that you don't need to experience a traumatic event in order to know that your life is awesome. I want you to discover that you are *already* awesome and you have amazing potential that is just waiting to be unleashed.

Everyone has *something* that makes them awesome. I discovered this while being one of the top coin dealers in America. The skills I learned in this profession helped me achieve more in my life than I ever thought possible.

Your unique skills can help you do the same.

When I was a boy, my father provided me with a cigar box of old coins he'd collected. I became a collector as well, and I loved it so much that when I was 17, I applied for that job as a bank teller because I found the idea of being around coins enticing.

At work, I searched the rolls of coins deposited at my teller window. I would often find wheat back Lincoln cents dating from 1958 and earlier, and, occasionally, a silver dime or quarter. Every day was a treasure hunt!

What I *really* dreamed of finding was a 1943 copper penny or a 1909-S VDB Lincoln cent. Those were the rarest and most valuable of the entire Lincoln cent series.

Searching for hidden treasure in coin rolls was thrilling, and the expectation of possibly finding something of value made it exciting for me to wake up in the morning and go to work.

Waking up every morning with a purpose makes it so much easier to be excited about your day. Are you enthusiastic about waking up in the morning and going to work? If you aren't, I want you to discover that you have unlimited potential, untapped abilities, unbelievable mental strength, and the resilience to become an accomplished human being (one whom others might someday read about). You won't have to go searching for your capabilities; you already possess them.

In this book, I will discuss the concepts that allowed me to become one of the top rare-coin dealers in the world. I will share with you the skills that allowed me to take control of my destiny.

When you start to realize that you have the innate ability to achieve great things in your life, you will completely change the way you see yourself. You will realize that there is no one as unique and awesome as you.

The way you look at yourself is who you will become. When you realize you're a living miracle, you will wake up every morning fired up to start your day!

Besides being a coin dealer, for many years, I've taught classes on relationships, motivation, and how to achieve one's potential. Many of the concepts I've taught are the ones that have allowed me to become a success in my field. When I started presenting these concepts in my classes, I was continually bombarded with questions about where more of this information could be found. This book is a compilation of the material from those classes.

The ability to become aware of how awesome you are is within your reach. This book will help motivate you to achieve everything you want in life and realize that you already have all of the tools you need. You don't need miracle drugs, creams, diets, foods, classes, or seminars to get what you want.

Most people go through life just *trying to get by.* If they can get through the day without major setbacks in their health or financial standing, they have succeeded. They try to avoid being late to work, getting caught speeding, being diagnosed with cancer, receiving a dreaded audit letter from the IRS, and now, catching a deadly disease just by walking out of the house. If we can get through life without hurting ourselves, getting in trouble, or getting sick, we consider ourselves a success.

However, that is not how life should be lived! Thriving in life comes from *striving to be our best,* not just surviving.

I think of it like this: each of us is given a "check" at birth that represents our talents, abilities, and potential. Our job in life is to cash the check and realize the potential we were given.

Can you imagine going to the bank to cash a $5,000 check and asking the teller to give you only $4,000? That would be absurd. In this book, my goal is to motivate and inspire you to cash your check *for its full amount.*

Life is fleeting, and if you are not living in the moment every day, enjoying every second, with the ultimate appreciation of the potential you were given, then you are not reaching the heights of bliss you are capable of reaching. When you start to blossom, you'll realize that you're awesome. So let's get started and discover how awesome you really are!

You Are Already Awesome

Do you ever wonder about how awesome you are and how much potential you have? Did it ever occur to you that you could achieve great things, but you just never thought it was in the cards?

Who would ever think that your hobbies or activities you enjoy the most could be clues as ways you could actualize your potential.

As a kid, I would play with my dad's coin collection. It was full of all sorts of American coins: large cents from the 1700s, silver dollars from the 1800s, unusual coins I never knew existed, such as 3-cent silver pieces, 20-cent pieces, and even a 2-cent piece. I played with them and pretended that I was back in olden times.

My favorite coins were dimes from the 1820s and 1830s, and, eventually, these were what led me to start collecting coins.

Little did I know that being a coin collector would lead me to become a coin dealer and enjoy this profession for more than 35 years. My mother never really understood what I did for a living and always asked, "When are you going to get a real job and be a lawyer like your father?" I didn't want to be a lawyer. Instead, I followed my passion and became one of the world's top coin dealers.

Many people want to achieve great things, but few of us think we can have it all: a strong marriage, a wonderful family, financial independence, meaning and purpose, amazing health, and a life filled with passion. These are all achievable goals as long as you realize that you are awesome. When this becomes clear, you will realize that you can be the greatest person possible and that nothing can stop you except yourself.

Imagine that after you die, you are able to read notes that had been made about your potential before you were born, listing all the things you were capable of achieving in your life. What if you find out that you could have cured diseases, negotiated peace agreements between warring countries, raised amazing children, or built successful companies that made the world a better place? How would you feel? Would you be upset with yourself for not having tried harder?

You are already awesome and have amazing potential; more than you ever thought possible. You just have to figure out what is holding you back from unleashing it.

You were born in the greatest period of human history. If you had been born in 1900, you would have had to endure the Great War, the 1918 flu pandemic, the Great Depression, and the Second World War. Things were even more bleak further back in history. Humans had lower life expectancy, that is, if they were lucky enough to have survived birth and made it to their first birthday.

If you are living in a first-world country, you're alive in the time with the best-ever standard of living. If you earn more than $30,000 a year, you're in the top 1 percent in terms of wealth. You're better off than the richest person in the world probably was less than 100 years ago.

How did you get to be here at this point in time?

You Won the Biggest Race in the World

Not only were you born at the greatest time in history, you had to win the most monumental race in existence. This isn't the New York City Marathon you had to win. You didn't have to beat out tens of thousands of runners. You had to beat out hundreds of millions of cells. When your parents conceived, there was a race to the finish line, and your sperm happened to win. Waiting there was your unique egg. If it had been a different sperm or egg, the unique person you are would not be here.

Start thinking from the perspective that your even being alive today is like winning the lottery.

Imagine you are reading a headline in your local newspaper that says the lottery was won by someone who purchased a ticket at the same convenience store where you bought your ticket. You run to check your lottery numbers, and to your amazement, you have the winning ticket.

How do you feel? Like you're on top of the world! Full of joy and excitement. What has changed between this moment and two minutes ago? Nothing, except the way you think about your future. At this moment, your checking account has the same balance, you have the same income and expenses, and everything else is *exactly* the same as it was two minutes ago. According to Stephen Baars, author of *Win,* only one thing has changed: your perception of the future.

Now imagine that you can wake up with that same excited feeling every morning without having won the lottery, but realizing that you've won the lottery that gave you life.

This is how I woke up every Monday morning, knowing that there was a chance I could discover an old cigar box full of rare coins that was being sold in a small country auction in the middle of nowhere. Every day was like playing the lottery because I never knew what surprise I might find. That excitement is what helped propel me to buy and sell coins with the largest coin dealers in the world.

Very few people think of themselves as awesome. Most believe *some other person* is awesome and "I'm just average."

Some people subscribe to a belief that it's impossible to reach their potential in life, become great, or do impressive things. This is where I want you to change your thinking. The word *impossible* is made up of two words, *I'm* and *possible.* It's a possibility that you can accomplish anything you want and reach your potential. As they say in New York City, "You ain't chopped liver!"

You're Not an Alien

Baars says that Carl Sagan and King David had an argument with each other, even though they lived thousands of years apart. Sagan, a famous scientist and astronomer who died in 1996, was convinced that the universe is so large that it must be home to other life forms. Applying logical assumptions, he calculated the possible number of advanced civilizations capable of interstellar travel as about 1 million. There was no evidence for this prediction; he was just making an educated guess. It wasn't as if astronauts found candy wrappers from another civilization lying on the surface of the moon. Satellites originating from Earth have never recorded another satellite or spaceship of unknown origin buzzing by. So far, there is no hard evidence of other life in the universe, just speculation.

Sagan's final assumption was that if, considering the vastness of the universe, there are no other life forms, then the universe is a complete waste of space.

King David, the second king of the nation of Israel, who lived more than 3,000 years ago, concluded *the exact opposite.* He said human beings are such a big deal that the entire universe was created just for us.

So, who's correct: Carl Sagan or King David? If King David is correct that the entire universe was created for us, then we should feel very special.

Great Things Come in Large Packages

It's your wife's birthday, and you are giving her a Tiffany & Co. bracelet she has always wanted. A truck pulls up to your house and the driver delivers a large box. Your wife opens the box, and inside is a smaller box. She opens the smaller box, takes out a bunch of fluffy material, and finds an even smaller box. She opens that to find a tiny box lined with silk fabric. Inside is a little pouch with the bracelet tucked inside.

A friend who's with her asks, "Why such a big truck and large boxes for such a small present?"

This is the same type of dynamic that King David is arguing about with Carl Sagan. Sagan said that if the vast universe has no other life, it's a complete waste of space. King David's implication is that the universe is so big in order to show the value of a human being. If King David is correct, which many scientists believe to be true, then that means the universe was created just for you.

That's the feeling you need to have in order to feel like you are awesome. I know it's difficult because humans have the tendency to feel very small. We tend to judge ourselves against others and their successes in life. We are just like that Tiffany bracelet: we feel small compared with the size of the universe. But that is the whole point. If we are the *purpose* of the universe, then we should feel very special.

You are so important that the day you were born it was decided that the universe could no longer go on without you. When you look at your life knowing how special you are, you will live with much more purpose and passion.

Imagine that your uncle, a diamond dealer, suddenly dies. You don't think too much of it because you didn't know him well and never made an attempt to have a relationship with him, so you don't expect him to leave you anything. You learn that he's left you a small black silk bag of diamonds. You are happy he left you something, but you have no expectations of it being of much value.

You take the diamonds to a local jewelry dealer, not thinking they're worth much, and he pays you

$5,000 for them. You are pleasantly surprised, but that kind of money is not life changing to you, so you don't think much of it.

Years later, you learn that the diamonds you sold were rare pink, red, and blue specimens worth tens of millions of dollars. You sold them for a fraction of their value for one reason: you assumed they had little value. You didn't consider doing research to find out their potential worth.

The lesson is: "Don't take life for granted." You are an important part of the most advanced species the world has ever seen. Not only are you awesome, you have the ability to do great things. You have the ability to live the life you always dreamed of, have a passionate marriage, and raise amazing children. Great things are yours to achieve as long as you realize that just as colored diamonds are rare and valuable, so, too, are you.

Hidden Treasure Everywhere

One of the benefits of being a coin dealer is that you can find coins almost anywhere in the United States. There are coin stores in almost every city, and coin auctions and trade shows occur almost every week. It's like there's hidden treasure everywhere.

One summer weekend in Maryland while driving to the beach with a friend, we stopped at a hotel to look at a few coins being sold in an auction. This was called a "secret" auction in the jargon of the coin business; it wasn't really a secret, but the coins were being sold by a very small, relatively unknown auction company, not one of the major auction houses.

As I was previewing the coins, my friend noticed that my leg was shaking and asked why. I told him that a number of the coins were worth considerably more than the auction catalog estimates of their worth. Not just hundreds of dollars more, *thousands.* No wonder my leg was shaking.

When the auction started, I looked around the room, and to my surprise, none of my usual bidding competition had shown up. I told my friend I could not believe that nobody was there to bid up the prices of these valuable coins. I was able to buy them for less than half of what they were worth.

My friend was amazed that I could just walk into an auction, raise my hand and bid, buy some coins, make a bunch of money, and then continue on to the beach.

Wherever I traveled, I would stop at the local coin store and buy coins. I always found coins I could make money on. This happened from Portland, Maine, to Las Vegas, Nevada. I don't think I had any special talent that other coin dealers lacked or that I worked harder than they did. I may just have been more passionate about finding hidden value.

Finding coins while driving to the beach or on vacation made me feel like a treasure hunter.

However, the most valuable type of treasure, something most of us take for granted, is right under our noses. I think it's safe to say that the greatest treasure is hidden within ourselves. When we can unlock those valuable gems, they will allow us to reach our potential in life.

It's What's inside That Counts

Many years later, I figured out why I could consistently go into almost any coin store and find a way to make money. These concepts became obvious to me when I wondered why other dealers were not able to achieve the same level of success I'd accomplished.

Here are my lessons learned:

Be extra nice. People like to do business with people they like. I wasn't always the dealer who was going to pay the most for coins, but people liked to do business with me anyway. Most people can tell if you are being genuinely nice or you're just putting on a ruse. If people like you, they will be more willing to negotiate with you, and you will more likely be successful.

I know this from experience: when I need to hire somebody, for instance, a contractor for a job at my house, I don't base the choice on the bid amount unless there's a considerable difference. If bids are roughly the same, I hire the contractor I like the most, not the one with the lowest bid.

Be trustworthy. At trade shows and conventions, I always wrote a check as soon as I made a purchase. Fellow coin dealers knew my checks never bounced and that I paid my bills in a timely manner. This endeared me to dealers because it was not always easy for them to get checks from people. They also knew that whatever I said was the truth; they never had to worry about being lied to. You would think that for most people, truth would be the default, but unfortunately, that's not always the case.

Don't be greedy; be flexible on profit margins. People are turned off by and less interested in doing business with people who seem greedy.

Some dealers won't buy or sell a coin unless they earn a certain profit margin. I am not saying that's wrong; there are situations in which you may rightly want to be firm on your price, but being flexible is a character trait that will get you to being awesome. Sometimes you have to be willing to negotiate and not be set in your ways.

Also, if you want to be at the top of your game in anything, it's better to do business with more people, because this can open up more opportunities. The more flexible you are, especially in your profit margins, the more that people will want to deal with you.

I was always willing to work on small margins, which meant I was able to do more business. This generally turned out well because many times when I purchased coins on which I could make a small profit, I would surprisingly end up making a large profit. There are a number of reasons for this, but the most common was that the price of gold or silver went up after I bought a coin.

I also never held out for the last dollar when selling coins, which meant that customers came back to do business with me. I don't have the desire to be the richest person in the room, but I will never be waiting in a soup kitchen line.

Don't be afraid to make mistakes. There's a saying in the coin business that "If you don't lose money on coins, you're not buying enough of them." It means you are being too conservative and missing out on moneymaking opportunities. The fear of making mistakes can stunt your ability to become good at anything. If you want to reach your potential in life, you must get over the fear of making mistakes. It's the only way to learn and grow as a person.

When I went to a coin store, I was aggressive in my buying. It's always better to try to buy as many coins as possible and leave the store having written a large check. Sometimes I would even buy coins I knew I could lose a small amount on just to make the check as big as possible. If a store owner knows you'll spend a lot, they will always welcome you back with open arms and more likely hold deals for you.

Just as there were hidden treasures waiting for me to discover, your greatest treasure is also waiting for you, right under your nose.

The Unfathomable Human Body

The human body seems mind-blowing if you take the time to understand its abilities. The memory capacity of the average adult brain is comparable to billions of megabits of information. The cerebral cortex, the outer part of the brain, has 125 trillion synapses (nerve connections). One synapse can store 4.7 bits of information. If the human brain were a computer, it would have the capacity of at least 1 petabyte and as many as 2.5 petabytes.

The entire Library of Congress contains 1 percent of a petabyte worth of books. This means your brain could store the material of more than 100 Libraries of Congress! Think about this the next time you're struggling to memorize lines in a play or study for a test.

If you could lay out all the blood vessels in the human brain from end to end, the length would measure more than 100,000 miles. That is like going around the Earth's equator more than four times! These numbers are difficult to conceptualize.

I was recently at a hospital to visit a relative who was having heart surgery. During the operation, he was plugged into a machine that continued to pump his heart. The heart machine was plugged into a socket in the wall, which was powered by the local electric company. In addition, the hospital had a back-up generator, and, most likely, a second back-up generator. When the operation was almost over, the doctors took his heart off of the machine and it started to pump on its own again. I thought to myself, "What's his heart plugged in to now?" The heart pumps on its own its entire life, with no electrical source? How is that possible?

A sinoatrial (SA) node triggers the electrical impulse that keeps the heart going. Where does that node get its power? Is it plugged in to a wall? Is there a back-up generator? I understand the scientific answer as to why the heart keeps pumping, but where does the SA node get its electrical energy? I have not been able to find the answer to this question. I don't remember having to change the batteries in my heart. If you think about, the whole thing is pretty awesome.

We take for granted many things in life. How is it possible that our stomachs, which contain acids to break down food, don't eat themselves up? How is it possible that a baby can grow inside a woman's body? How is it that we have microcomputers on our skin that can feel something without us seeing it? I could go on and on about our bodies, but this book isn't about human biology, it's about discovering how awesome you are. And you don't have to look very deeply at how your body works to realize that you are amazing.

One reason you may not feel awesome is if you have any disabilities that keep you from functioning at 100 percent. The next parable may help you change your thinking.

A Parable for Life

One day, a king noticed that his water carrier looked despondent, so he asked why he looked sad.
The man answered that every day, he carried two buckets of water on a pole that he balanced on the back of his neck. Unfortunately, one of the buckets had a small crack, and by the time he got from the stream to the castle, half of the water had leaked out.

The king told the water carrier to follow him down to the stream and show him the path he used. The king told the man he could tell which bucket had the crack: the one on his right. The water carrier seemed confused. The king pointed out that the left side of the path was just dirt and pebbles; completely void of life. The right side was alive and green with grass, plants, and flowers; full of life!

The king added that no matter how much water was leaking out of the bucket, the cracks were creating his potential. Without them, there would be no life.

No one is perfect. We all have faults and make mistakes, but we also have amazing abilities we may not even realize. The right bucket may have cracks, but it's those cracks that may also help you create an exceptional life.

Maybe you don't feel like you're awesome. Have you ever thought about what's keeping you from feeling that way? Do some serious introspection and realize that you have the ability to live an amazing life. Don't take the gifts you've been given for granted. You're a treasure waiting to be discovered because you are already awesome.

Unleash the Real You

Life is not about getting things; it's about becoming something.—Charlie Harary

The Palm Beacher

Many years ago, my wife and I purchased a small condo in Palm Beach, Florida. When we arrived to stay there for the first time one summer, I immediately went to a local store to buy clothes. I thought that if I dressed like a Palm Beacher, it would make me happy.

Where do you go for clothes that make you look like you're from Palm Beach? Marshalls? Not really. You go shop on Worth Avenue, the street with some of the most expensive clothing stores in the world: Chanel, Gucci, Armani, Ferragamo. It's very similar to Rodeo Drive in Beverly Hills and 5th Avenue in New York City. However, by buying clothes in the summer, when most of Palm Beach is empty and there are huge sales, I could take advantage of markdowns as high as 90 percent off the list price. I bought pastel silk shirts, white linen pants, a colorful jacket, and loafers (which I wore without socks).

After many years of dressing like an actor from *Miami Vice,* I decided that I wasn't going to wear these clothes anymore. I figured out that I was not trying to be the real me; I was trying to be someone else. I had thought that if I looked like a Palm Beacher, I would feel good about myself, and for a short while, I probably did. In the end, though, I was simply trying to be somebody I wasn't (especially Don Johnson). I was also trying to *be* great by *looking* great.

Our insecurities can make us try to be like others because we may not be happy with the way we are, *or* we think we'd be happier being like somebody else. Feelings of insecurity, fueled by low self-esteem and a need for approval, can take over. The thing is, our personal feelings are just our thoughts about our own reality, which may be distorted.

One of the most exhausting things you can do is try to serve up an image of what you think other people would like about you. The greatest prison we can put ourselves in is succumbing to the fear of what we think other people may think of us.

Wanting to look or act like someone else starts young. Just as I thought looking like a Palm Beacher would make me happy, the same holds true for children when they reach a certain age.

Asking a first grader to wear a warm winter hat when it's cold outside is usually not an issue. But around fifth or sixth grade, when children start to care what other kids think of them, they start to refuse to wear a hat. Kids think that how they dress affects what their friends think of them. Some would rather freeze their ears off than suffer the indignity of wearing a hat in front of their friends. They don't realize that *true* friends would not be judging them by their clothing.

There is societal pressure to maintain a certain lifestyle when people start to become financially successful. Whether you succumb to that pressure is up to you.

When my friend from college worked at a stock brokerage firm, he had to cold-call clients and try to get them to buy penny stocks. The stocks had high commissions, so the salespeople had lots of incentives to be aggressive and work long hours. The company management encouraged them to wear an expensive watch and drive a luxury car. Management wanted them to maintain an expensive lifestyle even if it made them go into debt; the idea was that being in debt would motivate them to work harder.

When someone becomes successful in the coin business, they may also feel pressure to fit in with their colleagues by wearing a fancy watch. Almost every successful coin dealer wears a Rolex. I thought I needed to wear one, too. Later, I realized that I had given in to expectations in the profession. Wearing a Rolex wasn't something that really made me happy. I needed only a watch that worked and looked nice, so I sold the Rolex and bought a Timex. Plus, it takes a licking and keeps on ticking.

Unleashing the real you means being the person you truly are and letting go of trying to please others. It's only when you are willing to allow your true self to emerge that you can live a healthy emotional life. This is what it means to unleash the real you: stop worrying about what others think and be authentic. When you can do this, you can free yourself of a great deal of stress and anxiety, and you'll realize how awesome you are just the way you are.

Finding Your Emotional Serenity

Many people have a fear of public speaking. Some would rather have a colonoscopy than have to speak in front of a group. It's because public speaking puts you on display and makes you vulnerable. You may be afraid of what people think of you, or of saying the wrong thing.

We seem to judge ourselves much more harshly than anyone else. When you can understand that being vulnerable is a way that you can achieve great things in life, it becomes easier to allow yourself to be vulnerable. You can then live with a sense of emotional serenity that eludes many people. Then, you can stand in front of a room of people with the confidence that you will do a great job, even if you don't.

Emotional serenity is the feeling that you are happy wherever you are in life. It's the ability to wake up every day with a smile on your face. No matter how bad things are, or how bad they appear to be, you know that everything that happens to you is an opportunity for growth.

No matter how good a job you do speaking, there will always be someone who doesn't like it. This holds true for almost everything in life. You can't please everyone, and there will always be someone waiting to criticize you. There are people who don't like my books (not *you,* of course). If I had to worry about what every single person thought of them, I would never finish them. You may as well be who you are and not exhaust yourself trying to please others.

Have you ever watched a video of yourself speaking? It can be very difficult. You may grimace as you see the nuances of every facial movement and speech pattern. I have a lisp, and seeing it on video is distressing for me. I am also bothered when I see one side of my lip go up when the other side doesn't. Yet, if you were to ask people in my audiences about it, they might not even have noticed it.

One of the first things you're taught about public speaking (or acting) is to not break the flow of your presentation by saying things like "Oops!" or "I forgot my lines." Many times I have been lost during a presentation, and I made sure to not tip off the audience that I was confused or had said the wrong thing. The audience had absolutely *no idea* I was lost; they considered it a theatrical pause or me simply gathering my thoughts.

If you happened to have had bad skin as a teenager, like I did, you may have become *very* self-conscious about the way you looked. Have you ever had a pimple sitting on the middle of your nose? It drives you crazy, and you may agonize over it for hours, yet no one else really notices. Some things are all in our minds.

The same holds true when it comes to how you think your clothing may look. I used to spend 10 minutes ironing a shirt until every little crease was gone because I was worried that someone would think I looked disheveled. Then, one day, I watched a friend iron a shirt. He ironed only the front and finished in less than 20 seconds. He said 95 percent of the wrinkles were gone, even on the back, and that no one would notice any that were left. That was an eye opener for me: whether you spend 20 seconds or 10 minutes ironing a shirt, rarely will anyone notice any remaining small wrinkles. The extra 9 minutes and 40 seconds of ironing was just me feeling overly self-conscious about the way I look.

Becoming Vulnerable

Rabbi Abraham Twerski shares an interesting fact about lobsters. A lobster is a soft, mushy animal that lives in a hard shell. When its body grows, its shell does not grow with it. The lobster becomes very uncomfortable living in such a tight space, so it sheds its shell (molts). When the shell falls off, the lobster becomes vulnerable because it has no protection from predatory animals, so it hides under a rock or reef until it grows a new, larger shell. The lobster goes through this process multiple times in its life.

When we feel uncomfortable or are in emotional pain, what do we do? What many of us *don't* do is figuratively "lose our shell" and allow ourselves to be vulnerable and grow. Instead, we go see a doctor, who may prescribe Valium or Percocet. These drugs get many people through the day to avoid feeling much pain. But some of us take such drugs *without having physical pain.*

Unleashing the real you—becoming the person you really want to be—requires you to shed your shell and become emotionally vulnerable. You cannot be real with yourself when you are trying to please others or be someone you aren't. Real growth occurs only when you are willing to be vulnerable. Be real with your insecurities and anxieties; tackle them head on. This reality punch is not easy, but it's the way to become awesome.

No one likes to be vulnerable. It's hard to say, "I'm wrong." It's hard to say, "I love you." It's hard to say, "I need help." It's hard to grow as a person and be the person you are capable of being until you can be vulnerable.

When I started to date my future wife, Ilana, I knew deep down, after just talking with her on the phone, that this woman could be the one I'd marry. On our second date, I knew for sure, but I could not tell her because I was afraid to be vulnerable. I wanted to tell her how I felt without mentioning the words love or marriage, which would make me appear prematurely attached and overly exposed, so I said, "I'm never leaving."

To become vulnerable and be your true self, you need to wipe away any self-doubt you've built up over the years and love yourself the way you are, with all your vulnerabilities. If you love yourself, you won't lose yourself to self-doubt and worry.

Transforming Negative Emotions

In Latin, the word emotion means "To move." You want to move your emotions from a place of negativity to a place of transformation, a place where you can unleash the real you.

We make many decisions in life based on how we feel emotionally. If you are emotionally healthy, you tend to make good choices and generally feel pretty awesome. When people have negative emotions, they may tend to compensate for them by acting out in certain ways.

There are three ways people may deal negatively with emotions:

- Venting
- Numbing
- Suppressing

These unhealthy ways of hiding true feelings can easily manifest as anger, anxiety, or depression.

In addition, some people use drugs or alcohol to mask their emotions.

Others hide their insecurity and compensate for not allowing their true feelings to emerge by continually laughing or making jokes. I have always wondered why some people laugh at everything said during a conversation. It's not that the conversation is amusing, it's that they are hiding their feelings behind their laughter. For them, laughter makes them feel more comfortable than some alternative.

You may have seen this firsthand in the brilliant comedian Robin Williams. Although depression wasn't the official cause of his suicide, one has to wonder if it played a part. The underlying reason was likely an inability to deal with his emotions.

Some people cover up their emotional pain with risky behavior. A person in emotional pain just wants the pain to go away. The fear of dying that most people have may be muted, so their behavior can lead to a drug overdose or a tragedy from reckless driving.

It is hard for someone to be happy with someone else if they are not happy with themself. This is a golden rule to understand before you get married. This may be one reason some people are continually going in and out of marriages. They think marriage will help them find happiness and emotional serenity. If you are not happy with yourself or you are not able to show your real emotions, not only will you be unhappy, you will be more likely to make your spouse unhappy, and this will just make your problems twice as hard to solve.

People who blame others for certain things may have issues with those same things themselves. The external world is like a mirror: problems you see in other people are often the things you need to work on in yourself.

Ultimately, you want to *transform* negative emotions and deal with them in a healthy way.

Obligations Can Turn into Opportunities

There is a way to transform negative emotions so that they will always be representative of the real you. The way you look at things is the way you react to them. You can look at anything that happens to you in one of two ways: it's either an *opportunity* or an *obligation.*

I have to go to work, *I need* to pick up my kid from school, *I must* clean the kitchen…these are all obligations. We look at obligations as painful burdens. We want to run away from them.

If everything that happens to you is an obligation, you will lead a life of unhappiness and everything will feel like a burden. If you look at everything as an opportunity, you will be filled with more energy and emotionally happier. This applies to everything that happens in your life: your job, home life, exercise, relationships, and even your purpose for being on Earth.

What you need to do is articulate the pleasure you will get from performing your responsibilities. When all is said and done, you will find that doing the right thing will be your greatest source of pleasure. Learn to focus on the pleasure you'll receive from doing the task. Use the awareness that you will receive energy from doing the task to help get you through it.

Always try to find the pleasure in why you are doing anything, especially something that is difficult. It will help motivate you to keep pressing ahead.

For years, almost every week, I got up at 4 a.m. to travel to coin shows. It was not easy to get up at the crack of dawn to catch a flight across the country.

It would have been very easy to stay in bed, throw the covers over my head, and go back to sleep.

I was able to keep up this early-morning routine because I focused on the pleasures that could be waiting for me: the joy of discovering a previously unknown variety of coin or a coin that was mispriced and had significant profit potential. I told myself I would regret all the opportunities I'd miss if I stayed in bed. Sometimes I got motivated by telling myself that if I didn't go on a trip, I'd hear about *someone else* buying a highly profitable coin. That was all the motivation I needed.

A person who is real with their feelings looks at a situation and instead of asking "Why me?", asks "What's next?" What other pleasures are waiting for me if I choose to do the right thing?"

Why You Should Never Worry

If you look at everything as an obligation, you will always be worried because you will be focused on the effort involved, not the pleasure you'll receive. Being in a continual state of worry will drain you of happiness.

According to Rabbi Gavriel Friedman, there are two things in the world you should never worry about:

- Things you *can't control.* Why? You can't do anything about them, so why worry about them?

- Things you *can control.* Why? You can do something about them, so why worry about them?

Whether you can or can't control something, it won't help to worry about it. When you're able to internalize this concept, you will be able to live without worrying about what people think of you, among other things, and you'll be able to eliminate much of the stress of worrying.

You want to transform your emotions from something holding you down to something that puts you in control of becoming the person you want to be. Gaining the ability to transform your emotions is not easy, but it can help you realize how awesome you are.

I thought looking like a Palm Beacher would make me feel good about myself, but I learned that in the end, I would feel better by being true to myself and not trying to be like somebody else.

I am more in control of my emotions and generally a happier person when I make decisions based on my desires, not on what I assume other people think.

Unleashing the real you means asking yourself if you feel good about yourself based on who you are, not on your appearance. If you don't feel good about yourself the way you are, ask yourself why. Are you behaving in a certain way to try to please others?

To cover up an insecurity? Answering this question honestly will help you be true to yourself and get on the path to feeling awesome.

Everyone has the ability to find their awesome. Stop seeking others' approval. Look at every situation as an opportunity instead of an obligation, focus on the pleasure you'll feel by completing tasks, and realize that worrying is a waste of energy. Allow yourself to become vulnerable and give yourself room to grow. Then you'll be ready to shed your shell and unleash the real you.

Humility: Your Secret Weapon

If I only had a little humility, I'd be perfect.
—Ted Turner

In 2017, there was a total eclipse of the sun across a large swath of the United States. Some areas went completely dark. What is interesting is that while the moon appeared to be blotting out the entire sun, the moon is just a speck compared with the gigantic sun. If the sun were hollow, you could fit more than 64 million moons inside it!

How is it possible that something so small could block the light of something so large? It's because the moon is 400 times closer to Earth than the sun—a situation not shared by any other planet and moon combination we know of. If the moon were closer to the sun than the Earth, we would not have even noticed the eclipse.

small obstacles that some people encounter in life may appear big to them, when in reality, they are tiny. This may keep them from feeling and being awesome, just like the moon blocking the sun; something comparably tiny being able to block something so large. The sun brings life to our planet. Don't let something small prevent your life from being awesome.

Learning to Be Humble

Becoming humble is the secret weapon you need to keep small obstacles in life from preventing you from knowing how awesome you are.

Some people look at humility as a weakness, but it is actually a strength. A humble person can suppress feelings of being egocentric and connect to something greater than themself.

The opposite of humility is arrogance. When someone is arrogant, it is difficult for them to open their heart and share credit for their success. They think only about themself and how they can get more of what they want. They don't want to change for anybody or acknowledge anyone else's participation. They don't live with an important mantra: *Your ego is not your amigo.*

Arrogant people do have the ability to change. However, becoming humble usually takes a disaster in their personal life, such as financial collapse or the loss of a loved one.

My Not-So-Humble Beginnings

I didn't used to consider myself an arrogant person. That changed overnight when I become a major buyer in the coin business. I was in my early 20s and the coin market was smoking hot. At conventions, I did several hundred thousand dollars in business in just a few days.

I was making lots of money every day. One day stands out in my mind. I flew to Dallas to do business with the largest coin dealer in the world, Heritage Auctions. It's the third-largest auction company in the world, behind Christie's and Sotheby's. In less than 10 hours, I did more than $1 million in business. Even I was impressed.

I became arrogant. Fortunately, my arrogance lasted only a short period of time.

I understand how young professional athletes who sign big contracts often have a hard time handling their money and fame. When you are raking in cash, your perception is that you will *always* rake in cash, but that's not true.

My father lived during the Great Depression. I learned from him that income can disappear very quickly. You may have an easy time supporting yourself one day, but the next, you may have a hard time putting food on the table. As a boy, my father had to help support his family, which at times struggled to feed themselves. He sold newspapers and ice cream on the National Mall in

Washington, D.C. My father always taught me to save money for a rainy day. Taking that advice saved me many times.

There were periods of time in the coin business when it was extremely difficult for me to make money or even sell a coin. Most dealers held out for the last dollar when selling coins, so when things got tough, they had inventory and no cash. I never held out for the last dollar, so I always had little inventory, but that allowed me to have money in my account. During those times, I could still be a major coin buyer of coins, generally at depressed prices, when almost nobody else was able to buy them.

When I was 24, I decided something that helped propel me to the top as a coin dealer: I told myself that I would never lie or be arrogant again.

This was a game changer. I started to increase my business exponentially. More dealers wanted to split large coin deals that they either could not handle financially or they weren't sure about, so they needed expert advice. I became the expert.

Besides being truthful and eventually humbled, I employed three skills that were instrumental in my business success. These skills are important not just in business but in life:

Become an expert in something. Find something you love to do and get really good at it. I was great at maximizing the value of coins, either by knowing who would pay top dollar for them or being able to improve them to increase their value, for example, by professionally cleaning them to improve their beauty.

Communicate well. When someone has partnered with you on a deal, they want to get continuous updates. Nothing is more frustrating than putting your livelihood in the hands of someone and having no idea what is going on. If someone brought me a coin deal, I would tell them what I thought about the coins and their potential. I would also discuss the potential down-side risks, the length of time it could take to make a sale, and who the ultimate customer might be. This put the seller at ease, and I would also listen to their insights.

Always be honest. This is not an easy thing to do in the coin business or in any business that involves sales. Every dealer who worked with me knew they would always get the truth about the profit or loss potential. When people know you speak the truth, they will likely entrust you with more information, and that leads to more business. Plus, knowing that you speak the truth is the best way to avoid feeling stressed when you go to bed.

Transforming myself from an arrogant person to a humble one transformed my life. I became a much happier person, which also made everyone around me happier. Plus, I was continually offered profitable coin deals that I might never otherwise have seen.

Humility Will Make You Awesome

Humble people see everything as a learning opportunity. They are open to new ideas and willing to admit they are wrong.

There is a stereotype that when men are driving and get lost, they never stop and ask for directions. It's because they don't want to admit that they don't know what they're doing. It takes humility to stop and ask for help. (Women generally don't have a problem asking for directions; they tend to be more humble.)

When someone becomes financially successful, they may either believe that they achieved it all by themself, or humbly realize that they succeeded because they used their innate abilities. This is a major key to discovering that you're awesome: being aware that you are just "cashing the check" you received at birth and using your skill to make a living.

I was given amazing vision that let me see coins better than most people. I was able to see imperfections in coins that others could not see. I finally realized I was just cashing the check I'd been given.

Humble people see their strengths and weaknesses as part of their gifts in life. Their self-esteem is built on their intrinsic value of themselves, not on what they think others think of them.

Humble people are not the ones who are loud and boisterous when they walk into a room; they don't need to try to compensate for feelings of inferiority.

Humble people don't need fancy titles at work, fancy cars, or gigantic houses that show off their wealth. They do not have a need for material things in order to boost their egos.

Being humble means using everything at your disposal to achieve what you want, and if there is something beyond your capabilities, not being afraid to ask for help. You are not alone in the universe, and receiving help or advice could make all the difference between success and failure. *Teamwork will make your dreams work!*

Humility Is Critical in Marriage

When you are humble, your only concern is about doing what's right.

I like to say that in marriage, sometimes you have to be wrong in order to be right—that is, to keep the peace. For example, you can argue with your spouse about something when you *know* you are right. You may wear them down until they admit you are correct; and you may even *be* 100 percent correct.

But do you win? Or does your arrogance alienate your spouse, and, after a series of arguments, weaken your relationship? You win the battle but you may lose the war. Sometimes you need to be wrong: to bury your arrogance and find your humility; to agree with your spouse, even if you know they are wrong. This is not easy for most people to do, and it's virtually impossible for someone who is arrogant. It may hurt your pride, but if you're humble, you won't feel the pain because you realize that preserving the good feelings in the relationship is worth more than the satisfaction of having your spouse admit you're right.

Being Humble Means Thinking for Yourself

Humble people don't always follow society's expectations. Their values don't necessarily reflect their peers' values. They think for themselves and make choices based on their personal beliefs.

I read an article about how women in some countries do not shave their underarms—this practice is considered normal and part of women's natural beauty. In the comments about the article, I chuckled as I saw that many women thought the practice was gross. However, other people were fine with it. (Julia Roberts has hairy armpits; who doesn't love her?) If there were a trend in the U.S. in which celebrities starting showing off hairy underarms, my guess is that the women who objected might change their perceptions.

Societal norms may change on a whim, but that doesn't mean you have to change your personal beliefs. Being humble means thinking for yourself, being strong in your beliefs, and not being swayed by societal pressures.

Years ago, being tan was looked down on in terms of social standing. People of means did not need to be out working in fields or building railroads;

their skin was pure white. Today, some people will do almost anything to look tan, even though being in the sun can cause skin cancer. Beauty magazines show tan models. The perception that being tan makes you more beautiful is perpetuated by societal pressure. When you can resist societal pressure, you're thinking for yourself, humble, and potentially more likely to achieve what you really want in life.

Some people base their self-worth on indicators like the number of "friends" they have on Facebook, when that is only one of many indicators of a genuine friend. Most of them are not involved in a meaningful relationship with you; they are just people you're connected with online.

Humble people place a high value on meaningful things, such as community, spirituality, doing good deeds, and a host of other things that don't necessarily bring them accolades. They are not thinking less *of* themselves but less *about* themselves.

When your life has more meaning, you will handle stress more effectively and have higher levels of physical and mental well-being.

To sum it up: humility is true inner strength, which will allow you to reach your potential in life and help you discover your awesomeness.

Open Yourself to Other Ideas

Being humble means you're open to others' ideas. It means you can be objective about information and you don't necessarily accept everything you're told; you do your own research.

Humble people make great co-workers because they don't dismiss others' ideas. If your employee has an idea that improves business and you're humble, you don't feel like they are stepping on your toes or invading your turf. Humble people make decisions based on what's right, not what's best for them. If someone disrespects a humble person or forgets to give them the credit they deserve, they don't wallow in self-pity or get upset. They have the inner strength and self-esteem to retain their dignity.

Humble people also have a way of making people around them feel good about themselves, even if someone suggests ideas that are not useful. While an arrogant person may dismiss others, a humble person can tell them that their idea isn't workable without insulting them or making them feel small.

I Thought I Was the Greatest…

When I traded rare coins for a living, I considered myself one of the best in the business. When I took on a partner in certain aspects of the work, I quickly learned that I knew much less than I'd thought. I learned that there are people who are *much* smarter than I am, and that my arrogance was getting in the way of my learning about new ways of making money. My business partner taught me concepts that I had never considered. It opened my eyes to the fact that I really *wasn't* that great, and that I needed to be open to new ideas.

Later in this book, I discuss that even if you *are* the best at what you do, someone better will always come along. If you're arrogant, you may overlook this inconvenient truth. You should always be humbly working on yourself.

Are You Living to Work or Working to Live?

Ask yourself this question: Are you working to live or living to work? Both are acceptable, but if you want to be awesome, working to live is a much better choice.

I loved what I did for a living. It would almost be a mistake to call it work because I enjoyed "treasure hunting" so much. When you love what you do, you are more likely going to be good at it. You also won't dread having to wake up on Monday mornings for work.

We generally associate what people do for a living with who they are as people. What's the first thing you generally ask someone when you meet them? Probably "What do you do?"

Some people find their job by accident or just "fall" into it. The job then becomes who they are; they don't put effort into defining themselves as anything beyond what they do for work. I know many people who have the financial ability to do what they want in life, but they have not found anything truly meaningful outside of what they do for a living.

This may become especially apparent in retirement. Without a job to keep you occupied, you may wake up one day and ask, "What am I living for?"

Don't let your job completely define you as a person, because then you are less likely to look for meaningful endeavors. Your job then becomes your life.

Living for a sense of meaning is critical because as humans, meaning is our greatest need.

- If you have children, how far would you go to save their lives?
- If your country was at risk of being destroyed, would you fight to save it?
- Do you have a desire to create something positive that will outlast you?
- When you die, do you want the world to be in a better place?

If you want to discover how awesome you are, figure out what you're passionate about. You may even be willing to die for a cause. When you know what you're passionate about, or even willing to die for, then you can really start to live.

Imagining the End Game

In Stephen Covey's book, *The Seven Habits of Highly Successful People,* he mentions a concept that can help you find your awesomeness: "People are working harder than ever, but because they lack clarity and vision, they aren't getting very far. They, in essence, are pushing a rope with all of their might." He says, "Begin with the end game in mind."

His is a business-oriented book, so you would think the end game would be what you do with your business when you get older. Do you want to go public, sell it, have your children run it, or let it fold when you stop working? But that's not what he's writing about. He means how do you want people to remember you? What do you want people to say at your funeral?

A friend of mine lost his 20-something son in a car accident. At the funeral, all the eulogies were about how he had made skateboarding cool again; skateboard this and skateboard that. I heard nothing about how he treated his brothers, his relationship with his father, anything he did to help other people. I felt sad that nobody said anything about him unless it had to do with a skateboard. It was like a shock to my system that we could live our whole life and accomplish almost nothing.

This observation made me think about what I wanted people to say about *me* at *my* funeral. I didn't want to be known as the equivalent of a guy who made skateboarding cool again.

Can you imagine going to a funeral and hearing only eulogies about how the person amassed great wealth? Hearing about how many cars and houses they owned and how many vacations they took would be ridiculous.

Living life imagining what people will say about you at your funeral is a game changer.

I realized that I needed to change my perspective from "Everything is about me" to "I want to help others whenever I can." I decided that I wanted to help as many people as possible and be a beacon of light to anyone I encountered.

One of my favorite sayings is "It's our job to change the world, not let the world change us."

When you live life focused on others and less on yourself, you will find that you have much more energy to accomplish things and be more awesome. You can be the person who makes everyone around you feel great about themselves. You can be the person who lives with meaning and purpose. You can be the person who wakes up with a fire in your belly to make the world a better place. Do you know how I know you have that potential? Because you are reading this book!

What Will Be Your Legacy?

When you die, you can leave your family money. However, a monetary legacy could be a cause of conflict. Wealth left to children is often wasted, fought over, or spent on attorneys' fees.

There are really only two things worth leaving behind when we exit this world: our children and our good deeds. Both are a reflection of what we did with our lives.

Envision how you want to be remembered so that you can work toward it. Program your life so you can achieve the results you want. *You are the programmer!* No one else can determine your legacy. Continually review your life mission statement and align your actions with it.

Ignite Your Engines to Get to Awesomeness

Have you ever been to a rocket launch at Cape Canaveral? It is breathtaking.

A rocket launch is a great analogy for living your life.

When the countdown ends and the ignition starts, massive flames shoot out of the engines. Think of these as representing the fire and passion inside you.

When the rocket lifts off, it appears to move very slowly because it has to fight gravity to get out of Earth's atmosphere. Gravity represents all the challenges you have keeping you from soaring higher in life. The goal is to get your rocket into space, where gravity is no longer an obstacle. You can then travel easily and efficiently.

When we can break free from all the things holding us back, we can fly through life with very little holding us down. We may go very slowly at first, but the farther we go, the easier it gets. When we start to understand what it means to be humble, we can then start to overcome challenges that keep us down.

Think about what humility means to you. Do you feel like you're living a humble life or do you have a constant need to be told how great you are? Do you buy material things like fancy cars or expensive clothes to impress people? To truly find your awesome, you need to be honest with your answers.

Humility will help you realize that your challenges are just a means to find how awesome you really are. Instead of struggling like a rocket blasting off against gravity, you'll be cruising like one that's made it to outer space. When you're flying that high, you'll see your potential from a perspective you never knew existed. When you reach the right altitude, you'll have the right attitude.

Always Be Moving Forward

*The only person that ever stumbles
is someone moving forward.
You don't stumble backwards;
you stumble forward,
and you never stumble when you're stationary.
So don't worry about stumbling.
Keep pushing it forward.*
—James Carville

If you want to discover how awesome you are, make sure you are always moving toward your goals. You can't get to where you want to be in life if you are standing still. As long as you are moving forward, you have a chance to succeed. When you stop moving forward, you lose momentum.

If what you are doing is not advancing you in the direction you want to go, it may not be something you should pursue.

Think about how you would react to someone who is not accomplishing something or making an attempt to move toward their goal. Are they making excuses? This may help you see a similar pattern in yourself that's keeping you from moving forward.

When you make excuses, you are not being honest and may be telling yourself little lies. Don't make excuses for why you can't reach a goal. Don't try to justify why you are failing. Take responsibility for your failure and you'll be a stronger person who is grounded in reality.

Instead of saying "I can't," learn to say "I won't." This clarifies that you *can* do something; you're just not *willing* to do it. Saying "I won't" emphasizes that you have control but are not willing to try.

Don't be wishy-washy. Be clear on what you want in life. Be honest with yourself and do what it takes to keep moving forward.

Know Your Goals

Every decision you make should be based on your goals. This is true for *everything* in life.

When I started understanding how to stay focused on my goals, I started to more effectively achieve what I wanted. Whether I wanted to form new connections with people, have a better relationship with my wife, or make more money, I kept the goal in mind when I made decisions.

The first step is defining clear goals. You can't move toward goals unless you know what they are.

The goal of a numismatist is generally to own the finest coins. That's a great goal if you are a collector.

After childhood, I switched from being a coin collector to a dealer. After that, I had only one purpose, which was to make money.

Sometimes, usually in an auction, I would buy a coin because I loved it, not because I could sell it for more money. My ego would take over and I would refuse to stop bidding. The result was that I usually lost money on the coin. That worked against my ability to move toward my goal of earning a living. I let my emotions get in the way, and that does not work well when buying coins, though it's a good thing for the consignor.

As a consignor of coins in auctions, it does not get much better than when two wealthy collectors fight over one of your coins in an auction, especially if the auction is live and both of them are present. They bid the price of the coin up past what it's typically worth.

Recently, I consigned a 1920 Mercury Head dime in an auction. It was in the finest known condition for the date; among the millions of 1920 dimes, there was none better. I had the price reserved for about $17,000. I did not attend the auction, and a few days later, when I looked at the prices paid, I saw that the coin had sold for $45,000! I loved it when a collector wanted to succeed in owning a particular coin.

From Keg Parties to Charity Galas

In college and after graduation, I threw keg parties. My only goal was to make each party as much fun as possible. Because that was my only goal, I needed only enough money to buy drinks and food. I didn't care if there was a cent left afterward.

Later, I got involved in planning fundraising galas. My thinking was that a gala is just like a keg party except that the attendees wear nicer clothes and eat better food, and the event isn't held in a moldy basement. This assumption was not quite correct.

I found it easy to get caught up in trying to make galas beautiful, fun, and inspiring. But I needed to focus on what I was doing and why I was doing it. After consulting an expert on running galas, I learned that the purpose of a gala was *to raise money.* That was it. Raising money had not been my goal in college, so I had to change my way of thinking.

Of course a gala should be elegant, but spending extra money on anything that won't bring in more money is not focusing on the goal. Serving the finest Wagyu beef would have been nice, but it wasn't going to raise more money than serving sirloin steak. When it came time to select entertainment, we could have spent more than $10,000 on a band, but instead decided that for $3,000, we would get one that was "good enough." We raised a decent amount of money, but if I had lost focus on the goal, we could have made nothing or even lost money.

In fact, many organizations stop putting on galas because they do not raise as much money as the leadership anticipates. The people organizing it want it to be the most beautiful event, but the organization just needs to raise money. The goals are not consistent.

Failing to define clear goals keeps many people from being successful in their work and personal lives. When you don't know where you want to go, it's hard to go toward it.

In my book *The Ten Secrets to Find the Love of Your Life,* I give an example of why it is important to be clear about your goals: if you're dating in order to find a marriage partner, you have a different set of parameters than if you're dating to have fun. If your intention is to have fun, you may enjoy a physical connection with someone, and that connection could lead to marriage. That might work out, but it might also mean you have a higher chance of having a difficult marriage. Why? Because when you started dating, marriage was not your goal, so you may have missed clues on potential problems in a long-term relationship. If marriage had been your goal from the start, you might have realized that a fun person you were physically attracted to was not marriage material.

When we don't have clarity on where we are going in life, it's like driving without a destination in mind.

Use Your "Personal GPS"

You can't get where you want to go unless you know where you are going. It is the equivalent of entering a destination in your personal global positioning system (GPS). In both driving and in life, declaring your destination will at least take you in the right direction.

Are you ever indecisive about which lane to get in when you approach a stoplight on a busy road? If you are like many people, you get in the lane you'll need to be in after the light.

I always get in the shortest line of cars—the lane with the highest likelihood of getting me through the stoplight faster.

I know many drivers do not like to do this. Many people get in the lane they will *eventually* need to be in *well before* they need to be in it, especially if they have to get on a highway on-ramp immediately after the light.

However, my tactic may help you get to your destination more efficiently. I like to get through the light the fastest way possible and *then* worry about where I'm going.

Why am I telling you this? I'm suggesting that when you practice this strategy while doing less-important activities, like getting through a stoplight, then, when you're doing more-important things, you will focus on getting to your destination in the most efficient way. That can help you move forward in life and find your way to awesome.

When you're driving at night, you generally can't see more than 100 feet in front of you, but does that stop you from driving? No. Most people drive at night even though they can't see very far ahead of them.

When you take risks or do something out of your comfort zone, just keep moving forward, as if you're driving at night, because you will get somewhere, even if it's not your original destination. Moving forward in life means sometimes being willing to take an alternate path or pivot to a new destination.

You may be wondering: "Why go somewhere if it's not where I want to go?" You may not reach a destination you originally intended, but it will be better than standing still and living a stagnant life. As long as you are moving forward, you can get to places you never thought possible.

The Byproduct May Be More Important than Your Original Plan

When you're trying to achieve something, you may not succeed, but the *byproduct* of your attempt may turn out to be more consequential than reaching the goal would have been. In many instances, when a company or inventor tries to develop something, their biggest success ends up being completely different than what they had wanted. You can call these situations accidents or luck, but they occur in the process of continually moving forward.

A perfect example is the camera in your smartphone. In the 1990s, NASA wanted to miniaturize cameras for use in interplanetary space travel. Its engineers came up with a camera on a chip, known as a CMOS sensor. The idea of putting a camera in a phone was not part of the plan, but today, CMOS sensors are in millions of smartphones.

In 1943, naval engineer Richard James was trying to develop a spring that would support and stabilize sensitive equipment on ships. When one of the springs accidentally fell off of a shelf, it continued moving, and James got the idea for a toy. Today, more than 250 million Slinkys have been sold worldwide.

Play-Doh was accidentally invented in 1955 by Joseph and Noah McVicker as they were trying to make a wallpaper cleaner. More than 700 million pounds of Play-Doh have been sold since.

During World War II, while attempting to create a synthetic rubber substitute, James Wright dropped boric acid into silicone oil. The result was a polymerized substance that bounced, and Silly Putty was born. It was even used by the crew of Apollo 8 to secure tools in zero gravity.

Audiobooks, which were originally created for the blind, have become extremely popular with people who like to listen to books while they drive.

Cornflakes, microwave ovens, and penicillin were all discovered by accident.

If something like penicillin, which has had such a profound impact on the health of humanity, was discovered by accident, think about what you could accomplish just by moving forward.

I learned this concept firsthand in my coin business. Sometimes my best deals were afterthoughts. I would laugh to myself that I was able to make such a good profit on something that I almost didn't care about or buy.

Once I was in a coin store that had just purchased a cigar box full of rolls of uncirculated pennies from the 1960s and 1970s. I didn't think these pennies had much value. I bought them all for a little more than their intrinsic face value, about $50. I figured I had nothing to lose. The box sat in my office for months, until one day, I decided to go through the rolls.

I never cared about coins from the '60s and '70s. I mostly dealt in rare, valuable coins from the late 1700s, 1800s, and early 1900s. What I did not realize is that some of the higher-condition pennies from those years could be worth hundreds of dollars each. I ended up selling dozens of those pennies for hundreds of dollars each, and I'd bought them for only one cent apiece! I found more excitement in turning pennies into hundreds of dollars than in some of my deals where I made considerably more money.

Another time, this happened during a real estate deal. I was involved in buying a property for the sole purpose of redeveloping it as a gas station or convenience store. When we bought the property, the old building standing on it was an afterthought. I considered tearing it down to save money on taxes while we tried to find a tenant. One of our partners convinced us to not tear it down. He said, "You never know if it will end up being needed for a tenant." His thinking proved correct. The *only* reason we ended up leasing the property was because the prospective tenant needed the building.

Life is funny. It is *so* important that if you want to discover how awesome you are, you keep moving forward. You never know where you'll end up. The more doors you open, the more good things can happen, and the more opportunities may present themselves.

As we discussed earlier, being clear on your goals will help you become efficient at achieving them, as you will see in the next example.

Winning at Blackjack (and Other Things)

In my younger years, I spent a lot of time in Las Vegas attending coin conventions. As you might guess, I also spent some time gambling.

There are some fantastic life lessons to be learned from gambling.

The first lesson is *Don't gamble.* It's a losing proposition. There's a reason that casinos are able to give away lots of free stuff to entice people to visit: you are almost certain to lose money while gambling. One tactic to entice you to stay is offering opulent guest rooms. In the lowest-priced room at the Venetian Hotel and Casino, every room has a step-down living room with floor-to-ceiling glass, electronic drapes, and a stunning view of the city. There are two TVs in the living area and one in the beautiful bathroom. I've always joked that I could live in the bathroom at the Venetian.

I do not gamble anymore, and I do not recommend gambling. However, if you are going to gamble, you need to have clarity on what you are doing, and you need to know how to have a chance of beating the casino. If you don't, you will have almost no chance of walking away a winner. Most people do not have this clarity, and that's why casinos make so much money. One of my mantras when you go into any financial venture is "You want to be the house." In other words, you want to be just like the casino so that the odds are in your favor and you'll more likely be a winner.

Casinos make more money on people who don't think about what they are doing and just casually gamble. If you do that, you may as well give your money to the homeless; at least they will get a nice meal and you will have done a good deed.

The lesson I'm about to share is an analogy you can apply to anything in life. I use Blackjack in this example because it's the casino game with the best odds for the player.

The Secret of Winning Streaks

You have almost no chance of winning at Blackjack if you always bet the same amount of money on each hand. The odds of winning a hand in Blackjack are slightly less than 49 percent, which means you have slightly less than a 50/50 chance of winning each hand. Those odds are just for one hand.

The small difference in odds may not mean much if you play a few hands of Blackjack, but it can make a dramatic difference the longer you play. The longer you play, the more likely it is that the very small percentage you have of losing on each hand will slowly eat away at your pile of money. This is why casinos base how many freebies (such as drinks) they give you based on your average bet *and* the amount of time you gamble. The more time you spend gambling, the more of a chance you have of losing money.

A system I used has worked, but even it is not a guarantee that you will win; it just gives you a better chance of winning. This system is based on the premise that if you play for a long time, you will have both winning streaks and losing streaks. Streaks can last anywhere from a few hands to 20 or more. When you're on a winning streak, you want to win as much as possible. (Disclaimer: When gambling at a casino, you will have more losing streaks than winning streaks. Sorry.)

When you are losing many hands of Blackjack in a row, if you don't change the amount of money you're betting, you will lose the same amount of money on each hand. When you are winning many hands in a row, what I am about to tell you will help you win multiples of what you would have if you had lost those bets.

If you win two hands of Blackjack in a row, double your next bet. If you win two more hands in a row, double your next bet again.

Keep going until you get to the maximum table betting limit.

When I played Blackjack, my goal was to *lose* the maximum limit because that meant I had *won* a *lot* of money on the way up! Eventually you are going to lose a hand, but you want to win as much as possible and walk away from the table before you lose.

I was gambling at the Bellagio Hotel in Las Vegas, and I was betting $100 a hand. This was when I was single and didn't have anyone relying on me financially. Like I said, I *do not* recommend gambling. The table limit was $5,000. Every time I sat down, I would say to myself that I hoped to lose a $5,000 hand. Why would I want to lose a $5,000 hand? You must be thinking I'm crazy.

How do you get to a place where you can afford to lose a $5,000 hand? You have to win *many* big hands to get to that point. You would probably have at least $12,600 in your pile of chips, with an additional $5,000 of chips still in play. What started as playing Blackjack with a few hundred dollars will have turned into you betting $5,000 on one hand. If you can get to the point where you can bet a $5,000 hand, you've already won a lot, and if you lose, you are losing the casino's money. If you could win a few more big hands in a row, that would be even sweeter.

If you can't imagine losing a $5,000 hand in Blackjack, you won't have the opportunity to lose it, which means you will never have the chance to make that much to lose. Remember, you are only getting a chance to bet this much because you went on a huge winning streak and made a lot of money.

I apply a similar type of thinking to paying taxes. I hope to write a big check to the IRS because that means I made a lot of money. Although you may spend a lot of time working on ways to avoid paying taxes, you may be losing the focus on the larger goal of *making money.*

Prolonging a Winning Streak

Winning streaks do not always last, so take advantage of them while you can. When you are on a winning streak, when everything is going well in your life, it can pay off to stay focused on what's working. Maximize your winning and minimize the amount you lose.

For example, when my wife gave birth to our first child, I was traveling for business almost every week. I was doing extremely well. I told her that all the traveling would not last forever, and that I needed to take advantage of the highly profitable situation while I had the chance. Looking back, I feel that my approach was the right one. I maximized my earnings during that time, and now that my business is less lucrative, I'm able to spend more time with my family (and on writing books).

The Importance of the Pivot

In basketball, there is something called the "pivot:" you quickly change direction and turn your body so you are partially blocking your defender, giving you a clear shot at the basket.

In business, some companies have been stuck in a brick-and-mortar business model and unable to pivot to set up an online presence. They've quickly lost customers to new, nimbler start-ups that have been able to efficiently pinpoint-market their products and grab market share.

A classic example has occurred in the taxi business. As a result of the advent of Uber and Lyft, taxi companies completely lost their edge and the prices of taxi licenses plummeted. Taxi companies could not pivot fast enough and were caught with their proverbial pants down.

Uber and Lyft made ride hailing so efficient that I can't help but laugh when I see a taxi. I remember being at a restaurant while on a business trip, having to ask the host to call a taxi for me. I had no idea when it would show up, where it was, who the driver was, the make of the car, the price of the ride, or how long it would take me to get to my destination. Now we can easily hail rides and we have all the information we need at our fingertips.

My favorite part is that Uber and Lyft use on-demand pricing: during times of high demand, when there are not enough drivers, the fares go up, which gives other drivers an incentive to come out and drive. If there are too many drivers or not enough demand, the fares go down, and fewer drivers are interested in working. This helps ensure equilibrium between drivers and riders. I love that efficiency!

In my coin business, I experienced a scenario similar to what happened in the taxi business. In the late 1980s, third-party authentication and grading made their way into the business and quickly became the way that coins were bought and sold.

Many old-timers refused to jump in to this new way of trading. They were not willing to pivot, and they eventually went out of business. The ones who gravitated to the new program continued to thrive.

This scenario is happening even now. Segments of the coin business continually go in and out of favor. You never know which part of the market will be hot one year, dead the next year, and then crazy hot again.

Until recently, dimes from the 20th century was one area of the business that was very slow. That quickly changed when two fairly common Mercury dimes from the 1930's sold in auction. A 1931 San Francisco mint dime sold for $270,000 and a 1938 San Francisco mint dime sold for $370,000! Although they were the finest known for their perspective dates, you can purchase the same dates in just a slightly lower grade for under $1000. These are considered ridiculously high prices for these coins. My guess is that those coins would have sold for less than a tenth of those prices a few years ago. Those prices may be crazy, but if you're a coin dealer and you don't try to capitalize on changes in the market, you will be left in the dust. Coin traders who are able to pivot and start trading on what appears to be a new trend in the market can still keep moving forward and make a lot more money.

There is a concept called price anchoring. The anchoring effect is a cognitive bias that addresses the common human tendency to rely too heavily on the first piece of information offered.

During decision making, anchoring occurs when individuals use an initial piece of information to make subsequent judgments. As new information becomes available and causes an increase in the value of something, but your bias towards a previously lower value doesn't change with the new information, you are price anchoring. This may have affected you at one time in your life, maybe when you passed up a winning stock because the price went higher than what you were used to seeing it trade for. Or maybe you didn't buy your dream home because you thought the price had already gone up too much and you weren't willing to pay what the market commanded.

Anchoring is a common reason that people don't advance in life. They get so stuck in their previous belief that when there is some sort of change, for whatever reason, they are cemented in their earlier expectations and not willing to move forward.

If you are not moving forward, you're essentially going backward. If you are not learning and growing, life will pass you by.

Don't get set in your ways and don't get anchored down. Ask yourself if your life is going in the direction you want. Are you clear on your goals, and are your decisions taking you where you want to go? Are obstacles, such as being stubborn, or emotional issues, keeping you from moving forward?

Be willing to change direction when you need to in order to move forward. Pivoting means you are not stuck; you're willing to try a new path. When you can pivot, you can get around roadblocks to achieving your goals and keep moving forward.

I always refer to this parable when I need some motivation to keep moving forward.

Teaching a Monkey to Talk

One day, a king asks one of his courtiers if he can teach his pet monkey to talk. The courtier says to the king, "It's impossible; monkeys can't talk!" The king orders the courtier's head cut off. The king asks a second courtier, "Can you teach my money to talk?" The courier answers, "King, a monkey does not have the ability to speak!" The king then has his head cut off. Finally, the king seeks out his wisest courtier and asks the same question.

The wise courtier asks the king, "How much time do I have?" The king responds, "Six months." The courtier agrees to do it.

The other courtiers stand around in shock. They come up to the wise courtier and ask, "How are you going to teach a monkey to talk?" The courtier responds, "I have no plans to be able to teach the monkey to talk, but with six months to try, anything can happen; the king could die or the monkey could die. What do I have to lose?"

When you're always moving forward, you never know what can happen and what opportunities will open up. The king could die or the monkey could die. Always move toward your goals because you never know where they'll take you. Always be willing to pivot and get to where you're going in the most efficient way. When you start to believe that anything is possible in life, you will realize that life is amazing and you'll find your awesome.

Time Is Your Gift

*Yesterday is history, tomorrow is a mystery,
and today is a gift, that's why it's called
the present.*—Bill Keane

Imagine that you're on a bus, and sitting in front of you is a young man. As the bus travels down the road, the young man starts to throw $5 bills out the window. When you get off at your stop, he follows you. He walks up to you and asks if he can borrow $5.

What do you do?

If you're like most people, you say no. If he's throwing *his* money out the window, why let him waste *yours?*

That's exactly what we do when we waste time; it's like throwing money out the window.

To discover how awesome you are, you must realize that every second of your life is a gift. When you use your time judiciously, you can discover new capabilities and accomplish more than you can imagine. This is true for everyone; we're all given the same amount of time every day. We can't buy extra time and we can't save it for later.

Don't waste time dwelling on the past or worrying about the future. Enjoy using your time to attempt to reach your potential in life *right now.*

What I'm about to say may not sit well with you, but it's better that I tell you my opinion about what is true and have you get upset with me than sugarcoat my message to make it politically correct. This way, I can sleep at night knowing that I didn't mislead you.

Here's my truth: Discovering that you're awesome requires deep introspection about what you're doing with the time you have in your life, and you may need to change some of your habits.

Think about how many minutes you waste every week daydreaming, killing time, or doing something mindless (you learn nothing from the activity and it brings you no inspiration). Mindlessly channel surfing for an hour is wasting time. So is surfing the Internet.

Being an Avid Sports Fan: The Ultimate Time Waster

One of my biggest time wasters has been watching the NFL pregame. Besides the weather and the injury report, what the pregame announcers are discussing means nothing. They are just talking because that's what they get paid to do. Who cares what Terry Bradshaw or Howie Long thinks about the 3–4 defense or the speed of a wide receiver? Let the players play the game.

Watching a game is also not the best use of time. I've been a Washington Redskins fan my whole life. I *lived* for the team. I traveled to away games and hosted game-watching parties when I didn't. During the week, I watched sports shows and anything ESPN broadcast about the team. Every morning, I read the sports section. I read every article about the team from beginning to end. I dissected the statistics on the previous game.

Fortunately, later in life, I started to examine what I was doing more closely. I asked myself why I was spending so much time and money on something that was taking me away from meaningful activities.

When you ask yourself deep questions and answer them truthfully, you may not like the answers. No one wants to discover that they are doing something that wastes their time or is essentially meaningless.

When I looked at my football habit, what I saw did not sit well with me. I didn't know any of the players personally and I wasn't related to any of them. Most of them were not from my school or my area; they had no connection to my hometown. If any of them had been offered a contract from another team for even a few dollars more, they would have immediately left, as there is no team loyalty.

Daniel Snyder, the owner of my beloved team, lives near the hospital where I had an operation years ago. Did he visit me while I was in recovery? No. I had been spending money on his team my whole life, traveling around the country to be at games, screaming my lungs out and wearing socks, coats, sweatshirts, and even underwear with the Redskins logo on them. When I was young, I even cried when the team missed the playoffs. You would think he could have taken time to visit one of his biggest fans!

At least when you go to a high school sporting event, the players may be in one of your classes; you may sit with them at lunch, or you may be friends with them, which makes watching games a bit more meaningful.

I asked myself: When I sit down on a Sunday afternoon, which takes up almost the entire day, and watch a game played by guys I don't know, who are not from my town, on a team owned by someone who doesn't care about me, what or whom am I rooting for?

I realized I was basically just rooting for the jerseys on the players' backs. I was spending my Sunday rooting for *laundry.* So I decided that I might as well save my money, sit in my laundry room with a beer and pretzels, and watch the washing machine spin around!

I thought about what I was doing with my time, worshipping a team that did not care about me and with whom I had no personal relationship. Imagine if I had used that energy on *anything* else. I could have learned a new language, mastered a new skill, made new friends, built a business, helped the poor and homeless, or volunteered for charitable organizations.

Many of us have lost track of how much time we waste rooting for professional sports teams. We have forgotten how valuable our time is.

I can still enjoy games by recording them to watch when I have downtime. This way I can waste less time, fast-forward through the parts that aren't worth watching, and spend more time with my friends and family.

The National Throw-Stick League

Imagine that every day, you see a young man throwing a stick up toward a tree branch. You notice that the stick occasionally stays on the branch, but it usually falls back to the ground. He does this for hours every day. You finally ask what he's doing, and he says he's trying to get the stick to stay on the branch. What do you think?

You probably think what he's doing is nonsense and he might be mentally unstable. Yet, if there were a professional sports league called the NTL, the National Throw-Stick League, whose entire purpose was to get sticks to stay on branches, you would think differently. The game would be played with a standard-size stick certified by the league. Different species of trees would be used during games, and there would be uniforms and rules like how many tries you get and how many points you get for knocking your opponent's stick off the branch. You would have team names such as the Texas Teaks and the Seattle Sycamores.

If this young man were to win the championship game for his team and be the most valuable player, you would consider him a celebrity and someone you want to meet. Yet, in different circumstances, you would think he's mentally unstable. Competition and the recognition of adoring fans, along with constant media attention, turn trivial acts—ones we would objectively think are meaningless and a waste of time—into things of great importance to many of us. And if you can get a ball through a hoop while standing 24 feet away at least 40 percent of the time, you are guaranteed to make $10 million a year in the NBA and be a celebrity.

I am not questioning the exorbitant amounts of money professional athletes make. If owners can justify those sums for talented players, that's the market. I love free-market economies, but I also don't need to waste *my* time because other people adore athletes and worship teams.

Let me give you another personal example of how our views of what's important can be distorted.

Our family hosts groups visiting from around the world for meals. They come to us to experience an authentic Sabbath (every Saturday) lunch in Jerusalem. On occasion, we have been invited to host teams that play professional sports in the U.S.

If we were offered the chance to host the baseball team from my hometown, the Washington Nationals, we would jump at the chance, especially if one of the best pitchers currently in the league, Max Scherzer or Stephen Strasburg, were going to attend.

Now compare this with our being invited to host the champion cricket team from Australia, which would have included their best player, Steven Smith. He's the highest-paid cricket player in the world, worth tens of millions; a celebrity. But I have to admit that our family would not have changed our plans to accommodate his team.

Why? After all, cricket and baseball are fundamentally the same thing; both are played with a baseball and bat.

An American may not care about meeting the world's best cricket player, and an Australian may not be interested in meeting the world's best baseball player. People feel privileged to meet a sports star from their own country but not from another country, even if the sport is similar.

Why would we not be interested in meeting an athlete from another country? Because we aren't exposed to the awareness that they are a celebrity. We would be less impressed to meet them because we're not exposed to media about them, so we can be more objective. An athlete halfway around the world is just someone who has the ability to hit, shoot, or throw a ball better than anyone else in the world. Their sport has no impact on us.

This is just one example of how our views of what is important can be distorted, which can, in turn, cause us to waste time. When I realized this, I stopped spending all my time rooting for a team.

This does not mean you can't stay up to date on a sport or watch a game, it just means you don't have to make the sport the number-one focus of your life. If you focus your life on a sports team, you will miss out on discovering how awesome you are.

Be the Gatekeeper for Your Brain

I finally became aware that almost all of what's on TV (or any screen) is not helping us be awesome. TV makes it so that you don't have to think. You can sit in front of a TV or computer screen for hours and not realize how much time is passing. And even though there are some good educational and entertaining shows, you are training yourself to do nothing else.

Instead, you need to be the gatekeeper for your brain, not letting the influence of television affect your potential in life. If you are able to watch less TV, you will be able to accomplish much more in your life.

Some people might say I'm brainwashed. I would have to agree with that assessment, and I believe that it needed washing. It was full of all the dirt, filth, and meaningless dribble that I allowed to penetrate it. Now that it is nice and clean, I choose what I put in it. I make every effort to allow only meaningful ideas to enter my brain. If it's not good for me or I am not learning or being inspired by it, I don't watch, read, or listen to it.

If I am on a plane, I usually read a book or write course material. If I happen to watch a movie, it better be a good one. I refuse to watch something if it doesn't make me laugh or inspire me. Unfortunately, most movies don't fit my definition of what is worth watching. I doubt that I would be writing books if I had a TV in my living room.

The more you watch TV or anything on a screen, the more you want to watch. The more you don't have to use your mind, the more mindless TV watching you may do.

It's no different than eating healthy food. The more junk food you eat, the more junk food you want. People who have healthy eating habits realize this phenomenon and try their hardest to keep junk food out of the house. The less TV you watch, the less you'll want to watch.

It's probably not often that you finish watching a show and say to yourself that you feel great. You may think the show was great, but how do you feel about yourself? Did you accomplish anything meaningful by watching it? When you view yourself as someone who wants to learn, grow, and reach your potential, you'll realize that watching TV won't bring you the satisfaction it may have at one time.

In order to discover how awesome you are, you must be the gatekeeper for your brain. If what you put into your brain is mindless rubbish, you are wasting precious time.

Don't Be like Martin

I used to go to New York City a few times a month for rare coin auctions. My biggest competitor for many years was a dealer named Martin. He was extremely driven and I could never understand how he worked so hard. On a Sunday, he would drive from Boston to New York City, then look at the coins in the auction on Monday, Tuesday, and Wednesday. He would bid on the coins in person on Tuesday and Wednesday night, and the auctions would sometimes last until 1 a.m. He would spend Thursday processing his purchases. On Friday, he would go to a coin-grading service and wait for the coins to be graded. He would pick up his coins, drive home, and arrive in Boston late Friday night.

I, on the other hand, would go to New York early on a Tuesday, pay someone to bid for me on both nights of the auction, then arrive home on Tuesday night. I would have the coins I purchased shipped to me the following week. Same event, yet he was away from home for six days, and I was away from home for one. I suggested that he stop working so hard and spending so much time away from home.

Martin ended up getting divorced and losing his family in the process, then losing his wealth, and, eventually, his life.

You cannot replace the time you spend with loved ones. If you have children, the time you spend with them is directly correlated with how well adjusted they become. The more time you give your children, the more emotionally grounded they will be.

There's Never Enough Time

Many of us have become enslaved to being busy. We feel like we do not have enough time. We have trained ourselves to be busy and on the go without thinking about it. Some of us are even busier on weekends. We spend Saturday at the office to catch up. We go shopping or to sporting events. We keep ourselves so busy that we can't just enjoy peaceful moments without distractions.

When I worked at an office, I occasionally got a call on my cell phone when I was cleaning up my desk. I would tell the caller that I would call them from my car; I was so busy that I could talk to them only while I was driving.

We are so used to being busy that when we have a day off, we feel that we must go somewhere and sit in traffic. It's hard for us to just be at home and enjoy family time. People love to go on vacation because it takes them out of their normal routines, but even on vacation, they may stay very busy.

Texting has become popular because you can send a message without taking the time to talk on the phone. I love texting because of its efficiency, but has it given us more time?

Our expectations of how fast things should happen have changed so much that if it takes us more than two seconds to open an email, we start complaining that the Internet is too slow. (When your Internet service stops working, why is it always the worst time for it to go down?)

If there are more than three people in the check-out line at the grocery store, we start to fume.

Starbucks spends a fortune trying to reduce the customer's wait time by just a few seconds. There is a whole industry whose purpose is to reduce the time it takes a barista to sell and make a cup of coffee.

In homes, people used to need to hand-wash clothes, hang them up to dry, and sweep up dirt. Now we have time-saving devices like washing machines, dryers, and vacuum cleaners, but we are still busier than ever.

Making the Most of Your Moments

What if it were possible to slow down the Earth's rotation so that instead of having 24 hours a day, you had 28? Do you think you would still be busy?

If you think you would, you may not be using your time wisely.

One way that people misuse time is by not enjoying what they are doing. For instance, they order a juicy steak at a restaurant and then eat the entire thing in a few minutes. That is what a glutton does, not a connoisseur. A connoisseur enjoys every bite, gets pleasure from the texture, and doesn't rush through the meal.

When you view time as a gift, not as something unlimited, you will treat it as precious and try to enjoy every second.

Savor every second and don't rush through life without enjoying its pleasures. Learn how to stop and enjoy life for the sake of life itself.

The ability to stop what you're doing is a skill that takes some practice, but the rewards are worth it.

Remember that *we are not human doings, we are human beings.* The way to live an awesome life is to learn how to just *be.*

Start taking control of how you use your time. Learn to stop and enjoy each moment. You can't control the past or the future; you can only control the present, so focus on that.

No one gets to the end of their life and thinks, "I wish I'd spent more time at the office." They may wish they'd spent more time living life. If you are working on a Friday afternoon and have a pile of work on your desk, realize that no matter what happens, there will likely be more work on Monday morning, so you are better off taking a break and enjoying life.

If you are *doing this to get that* instead of *doing this and living that,* you are not in control of how you use your time.

If you want to get out of the trap of being busy and realize how awesome your life is, *Do this, live that.* Be in the moment, enjoying every day, making the most of everything you do.

What We Can Learn from Thanksgiving

I sometimes ask my students what their favorite holiday is. The majority of the time, they say Thanksgiving. I ask why. Their answers are similar: getting to spend time focusing on friends and family, and it's a day off to enjoy great food and take pleasure in being grateful.

Thanksgiving is similar to a holiday that people of the Jewish faith celebrate called Shabbat. They observe it every Friday from sundown until Saturday night. It's the one time in the week when many of them eat together without distractions from phones, computers, shopping, work, or obligations. They dress in beautiful clothes, eat a delicious meal, and focus on being grateful for things like spending time with family and friends. They are lucky, or some say blessed, to enjoy the same experience of the Thanksgiving holiday on a weekly basis, not just once a year.

Why do Americans celebrate Thanksgiving? Because President Lincoln created a national holiday so we could take a day off and be thankful. Here is part of the speech he made on October 3, 1863:

> The year that is drawing towards
> its close, has been filled with the
> blessings of fruitful fields and healthful
> skies. To these bounties, which are so
> constantly enjoyed that we are prone
> to forget the source from which they
> come, others have been added, which
> are of so extraordinary a nature, that
> they cannot fail to penetrate and soften
> even the heart which is habitually
> insensible to the ever watchful
> providence of Almighty God.
> I do therefore invite my fellow
> citizens in every part of the United
> States, and also those who are at
> sea and those who are sojourning in
> foreign lands, to set apart and observe
> the last Thursday of November next,

as a day of Thanksgiving and Praise to
our beneficent Father who dwelleth in
the Heavens.

It doesn't matter if you're Christian, Jewish,
Muslim, some other faith, or not religious. Everyone
needs a day to recharge; to unplug from the nonstop
world. Then, when you start the next week, you are
refreshed and ready to take on life with a new sense
of energy and efficiency.

You don't need to wait until Thanksgiving to take
a day off. Start taking a day off every week, and you
will gain control of your time.

Learning How to Stop

If you have ever been skiing, do you remember what
the first day was like? I remember how miserable I
was on my first day. The weather was cold, wet, and
windy, but the worst part was that I had no ability to
stop, which was frightening.

The first thing ski instructors teach beginners is
something called the "pizza:" keeping the tips of your
skis pointed at each other to make a triangle-shaped
wedge. This keeps you from going too fast and helps
you stay in control. As you get better at skiing, you
straighten out your skis and keep them parallel in a
position called the "french fry."

The more comfortable you get doing the french
fry, the easier it is to do the hockey stop, in which

you quickly dig your parallel skis into the snow and come to an immediate stop, even on a steep slope.

Before you are able to stop on skis, you most likely ski in fear because you don't have the ability to stop when you want. Skiing is a metaphor for life. When you have no control over your ability to stop being busy, you may fear what it is like to not be busy.

What would happen if you took a day off with no distractions such as the Internet? Many people are scared to find out that they could get more meaning and pleasure out of their lives.

What happens when you learn the hockey stop on skis and can then stop on a dime whenever you want? The entire mountain, which you may have been scared to ski, becomes your playground. Instead of being afraid of skiing, it is now a thrilling sport.

In the same way, knowing how to stop in life, on your terms, will fundamentally change how you live. You'll no longer be scared of taking a day off without distractions.

Do you use your time efficiently? Are you always busy and on the go? What would happen if you stopped watching so many TV shows or movies?

Think about all the amazing things you could do if you created more time for yourself. Consider letting go of activities that you *think* are important but that don't really reflect your values. It was not easy for me to realize that I had been wasting many hours on my local football team. When that became clear, my whole life opened up and I was able to discover who I really was.

Time is our most precious resource. You can't buy more time and you can't save time for later, but you can control how you use your time. Living a life in which you can stop whenever you want? That's a step toward discovering how awesome you really are.

Know Your Purpose

Many persons have a wrong idea of what constitutes true happiness. It is not attained through self-gratification but through fidelity to a worthy purpose.—Helen Keller

Can you think of anything in the world that was created without a purpose?

It's unlikely. Even mosquitos have a purpose. The larvae of mosquitos are food for fish and other wildlife, including larger larvae of other species, such as dragonflies. Larvae eat microscopic organic matter in water, helping recycle it. Adult mosquitos make up part of the diet of some insect-eating animals, including birds, bats, dragonflies, and spiders. They also help pollinate some flowers when they consume nectar. Although most of us hate mosquitos' annoying bites, mosquitos serve a purpose.

When you get clarity that this phenomenon includes *you,* you will start to realize how awesome you are, especially if you are able to fulfill your purpose. When you understand and know your purpose, everything you do in life will be more enjoyable and meaningful.

When you don't know your purpose for doing something, you will not enjoy it nearly as much. For example, think of children learning math. Many of them have a hard time learning something if they don't understand its purpose.

It may be difficult to see why some things have a purpose, but that doesn't mean there isn't a purpose, even for something like dangerous wild animals.

Wolves in Yellowstone Park

In the 1920s, local farmers succeeded in killing every wolf in Yellowstone National Park. What was once a major part of the ecosystem disappeared. Although local farmers were happy because they had stopped losing livestock, scientists and ecologists noticed that the park was declining. Although elk were still preyed on by bears, cougars, and coyotes, the absence of wolves took a huge amount of predatory pressure off of the elk.

As a result, the elk population thrived—*too well.* Two things happened: the elk pushed the limits of Yellowstone's capacity, and they didn't move around much in the winter. The elk didn't have to fear wolves, so they hung around the river beds grazing heavily on young willow, aspen, and cottonwood trees.

When the elk reduced the vegetation along the riverbanks, the banks began to erode and the rivers widened. The temperature of the rivers warmed because there was no shade cooling the water, so the abundance and distribution of fish species changed. Birds that lived near the river no longer had a riverbank on which to build their nests. The number of eagles that fed on the fish declined. Beavers had used willow trees on the riverbanks to make their dams, but because of the elk, there were no more willow trees, so they disappeared.

Many decades after the decimation of wolves in the park, the park service discussed reintroducing them. Bringing back the wolves struck a nerve among ranchers, but wildlife biologists felt that the wolves played a key role in the ecosystem, including in controlling the elk population, which had ballooned in the wolves' absence and wreaked havoc.

So, in 1995, eight gray wolves from Jasper National Park in Alberta, Canada, were allowed to roam Yellowstone. By the end of 1996, 31 wolves were brought in to the park.

The reintroduction of wolves balanced out the Yellowstone ecosystem. Yellowstone is thriving because what was once thought of as a dangerous animal is now considered a vital part of the ecosystem.

Wolves are causing a trophic cascade of ecological change, including helping increase beaver populations and bring back aspen trees and vegetation.

Who knows what would happen if we were able to completely wipe out the mosquito? If you love to barbecue, their extinction might make you very happy, but based on the wolf example, the unknown consequences could be devastating.

If wolves and mosquitos have purposes, if indeed, every creation on Earth has one, do you think your purpose is any less significant? Is your purpose similar to that of a tomato plant or a shark? Probably not. You have a different purpose for being on this planet.

There may be some questions that some of us ask later in life. We go to college so we are able to get a good job. Then we spend decades working so we can pay off student loans, mortgages, and cars. Then we retire, wondering what we did with our life. Did we spend it working to pay off our debts? Did we spend it trying to acquire money and material things? Could attaining financial freedom have been our only purpose? Was it to *do this so you can get that?*

Let's dig deeper. You can use logic to try to identify your purpose in life. When you have clarity on what you are *supposed* to be doing, you can live a more fulfilled life and make decisions based on your true purpose.

Let's go back to the beginnings of the universe.

The Big Bang Theory (*Not* the TV Show)

The Big Bang theory is a scientific explanation of how the universe began. Scientists believe the universe as we know it started with a tiny dot known as a singularity. The Big Bang was the eruption of this dot. Nothing became something, which inflated over the course of the next 13.8 billion years to become the cosmos of today. Anything that exists today, including humans, came from that original expansion.

Scientists called it the Big Bang because if they had called it what it technically was, creation, that would have implied the existence of a creator. Many scientists don't believe in the concept of a creator because there is no scientific way to explain it. There is much that can't be explained rationally: what triggered the Big Bang, how did the first cell appear, and how is it that everything in the world was designed so perfectly? There are many things in the world that scientists know exist but they can't see, such as radiation, microwaves, gravity, gluons, Oort clouds, black holes, magnetic fields, consciousness, radio waves, and air.

Science is a systematic enterprise that builds and organizes knowledge in the form of testable explanations and predictions about the universe. When there is no way to test something, it is just a theory. The evidence pointing to a creator is based on theory because we can't test it. There are many things in the world that we believe exist even though we can't test them, and the Big Bang is one of them.

We are familiar with theory and circumstantial evidence from our court system. In many court cases, someone is found guilty through circumstantial evidence. The best-known case is the O.J. Simpson murder trial. Even though he was found not guilty, many people believe he was guilty. Yet, no weapon was found and no one saw him murder anyone.

When there is enough circumstantial evidence pointing to a creator, cognitive dissonance may kick in, creating an opposition to what one perceives as threatening. The existence of a creator may require an obligation to that creator, which may make some people very uncomfortable.

The Creation of a Plastic Cup

What if I told you there was an explosion on Madison Avenue in New York City, and from this explosion, right out of thin air, came a plastic cup? You would say that's impossible. You might think I was crazy and throw this book out the window.

It's not possible for a plastic cup to come out of an explosion when a plastic cup previously didn't exist. Why? You would logically conclude that a plastic cup must be created and designed by someone. A plastic cup cannot spontaneously emerge from nothing.

If the design of a plastic cup is fairly simple, then the design of a smartphone, something infinitely more complicated, must have a more intelligent designer.

If something as simple as a plastic cup can't appear randomly out of an explosion, how can something infinitely more complicated, such as a human being, appear from the Big Bang? There is only one difference between the instant appearance of a cup from an explosion and the formation of humans millions of years after the Big Bang: the time scientists say it took for humans to evolve from a common ape ancestor of the chimpanzee. If time is the only constant needed for anything to have the possibility to develop, then there are two points that seem to refute that notion. (*Constant Connection,* R. Yitzchak Coopersmith, 2016.)

In his book *A Brief History of Time,* physicist Stephen Hawking says:

> It is a lot like the well-known hoard of monkeys hammering away on typewriters—most of what they write is garbage, but very occasionally by pure chance they will type out one of Shakespeare's sonnets. Similarly, in the case of the universe, could it be that we are living in a region that just happens to be by chance smooth and uniform?

In response to Hawking, fellow physicist Gerald Schroeder, in his book, *Genesis and the Big Bang,* calculated the odds of monkeys randomly typing an average Shakespearean sonnet. He chose the one that opens, "Shall I compare you to a summer's day?"

There are 488 letters in the sonnet. The chance of randomly typing these 488 letters in the same order is represented by the number 10^{690}, or 1 in 26^{488}. This is the same as in 1 in 10 followed by 690 zeros.

The immense scale becomes even more significant when one considers that if we use 15 billion years as the time since the Big Bang, only 10^{18} seconds have ticked away since then.

This is where the chances of this happening get more outrageous. If you could take every monkey in the world, plus all other animals that exist, give them each a typewriter, and let them try to randomly put together a 16-letter sentence (*not* a 488-letter sonnet), at one try per second, it would take 2 million billion (1 quintillion) years.

Let's disregard this argument based on Stephen Hawkins's theory.

Then there is the argument that cells were spontaneously generated on Earth.

Nobel laureate Sir Fred Hoyle calculated the odds of a bacterium spontaneously generating by itself. At first, Hoyle and his colleague Chandra

Wickramasinghe endorsed spontaneous generation of cells as a reason for the formation of life on Earth. It is impossible for life to exist without cells. After trying to calculate the odds of that happening, he backtracked on his claim that a cell, which needs about 2,000 enzymes to form, would ever be able to form by itself. He calculated the odds of that happening at 1 in 10 to the 40,000th power.

Yes, that number is hard to conceptualize. Here are some facts to help you put it in perspective:

- 1 in 10 to the 50th power quantifies the chances that mathematicians generally agree have zero probability of ever happening. Nada, zippo, zilch!
- 1 in 10 to the 67th power represents filling the entire state of Texas 50 feet deep in silver dollars. (That's about five stories' worth of silver dollars covering 270,000 square miles.) If you put your initials on one of them, these odds represent the chance of your picking out your silver dollar, blindfolded, on the first attempt.

Hoyle claimed: "The notion that not only the biopolymer but the operating program of a living cell could be arrived at by chance in a primordial organic soup here on the Earth is evidently nonsense of a high order."

He claimed that panspermia was the only way cells could exist on Earth. Panspermia is the theory that life came from outer space, either through space dust, space rocks, or aliens in spaceships. Panspermia doesn't explain how cells formed *someplace else.* His theory states that it is impossible for cells to emerge by themselves. He claims that the chance of even the simplest cell forming on Earth, without help from some other source, is the same as a tornado spinning through a junkyard and assembling a Boeing 747 jetliner from the random materials lying around.

Just to clarify, you need to be honest with yourself and not let your self-interest get in the way of what appear to be some basic principles of life. If we became humans by accident or were randomly formed from an explosion, even after billions of years, that means we are random beings created with no purpose. Either everything in the universe is a random occurrence, which means everything is an accident, or nothing is random. It can't be both!

Wouldn't it seem logical that since we are the most complex species in the known universe, nothing even close to a plastic cup or a smartphone, that there is a strong possibility we were designed? And if we were designed, what is our purpose for being designed the way we were?

It is much easier to think you just evolved randomly from a primate. It allows you to live life not worrying that you are not reaching your potential or fulfilling your purpose. Having no purpose gives you permission to fail. Having permission to fail allows you to go through life not reaching your potential and allowing yourself to never realize how awesome you really are.

The Four Levels of Creation

A concept from ancient Judaic writings dictates that there are four levels of creation:

- Water
- Plants
- Animals & Insects
- Humans

The higher levels cannot survive without the lower ones. Water is the foundation of life on Earth; without it, a living being cannot exist. That is why scientists and astronomers are always searching for signs of water or clues that it once existed on other planets.

Water has a purpose, which is to feed plants, animals, and humans. With water, plants flourish, providing nourishment to animals and humans. Animals have a purpose, which is to help humans. Humans use animals for food, clothing, and fat for cooking. In earlier times, animals were used to help people travel and plow fields. Insects are integral, too: without their pollination, Earth's ecosystem would not survive.

What is the purpose of humans? Would it make sense that everything else has a purpose but people don't? Using this logic, it would appear that we exist for some purpose.

Procreation: Fulfilling Our Ultimate Purpose

Of our many natural desires and instincts, there is one that we can survive our entire life without experiencing. Our natural desire to procreate may be the defining goal of our life, even if we don't end up having children.

We need food for energy; if we don't eat, we don't survive. We need water because we are thirsty. If we don't drink it, we will die. If we don't have air to breathe, we won't last but a few minutes. Yet, procreation is one thing we desire that we can survive without.

Eating, drinking, and breathing can't really be our purpose for living because we must do them to survive. Do any of these desires compare with the pleasure we get from the act that creates a baby? Eating is great, but I have never tasted a steak that could be *that* good.

So if making a baby is *that* good, should giving birth be even better? Not quite.

The Joys of Parenting Aren't Always So Joyous

Parents feel a lot of joy when having a baby, especially if it's their first child. Why? If they realized what they were going to put themselves through, I am not sure they would be so thrilled. At a minimum, it's at least a year of very little sleep, dirty diapers, spit-up on your clothes, and a complete change in your lifestyle.

The reason for parents' joy is their expectation of future happiness. If you look at childbirth and the first year after a baby is born, it isn't such fun. It can be miserable if you don't have the right mindset.

If the government said that after one year of birthing and then raising a baby, it would be taken away from you forever, do you think you would have children? It's not easy to say yes because the joy of having children is in watching them grow. If you had to have all of the pain of raising a child with none of the rewards, you probably wouldn't do it.

What is driving people to have children? We have an instinct that gives us the desire to procreate. The desire is so strong that some couples who are not able to have children still choose to adopt.

The reason we want children is so we can be givers. Giving is our ultimate purpose. However, you can still be a giver and fulfill your ultimate purpose without having children.

How Do We Know We Want to Be Givers?

Children are helpless when they come out of the womb to the point that parents *must* be givers in order for them to survive. Baby humans are unlike many mammals that are born with the ability to walk and eat on their own.

Would you ever consider asking your children to pay you back all the money you put into raising them? Of course not! Part of raising them is giving to them. Can you imagine giving your 21-year-old an invoice: "Here son, you owe Mommy and me $328,000. You can pay us back over the next 10 years. We'll only charge you 3 percent on the balance." That would be absurd. We don't *want* them to pay us back, that would take all the pleasure out of it!

What Do You Want for Your Children?

Most people say they want their children to be happy and healthy. They also want them to be good people, nice to others, to have happy marriages, and to raise healthy and happy children themselves. These desires are natural, so there has to be more to this.

Ultimately what you may want *from* your children is a relationship, one based on mutual loving respect for each other, not dysfunction. You want the relationship to be a healthy and joyous part of your life. If your children moved far away and you rarely saw them, you would certainly survive, but would you be happy? You would not be too happy because you would miss them. You want them to be a part of your life because you want to continually give to them, and to their children.

While raising my children, I discovered a clue that may have put everything together for me.

We Love Those Who Love Our Children

When my wife and I were raising our kids and we went out in the evening, we had to get a babysitter. Who were our favorite babysitters? The ones who gave our little ones the most time and attention. It is easy to find teenagers who will sit on the couch and play with their smartphones. We sought out the ones who interacted with our children.

The same goes for anyone who comes into our lives. Our favorite people are those who give to our children, whether by playing games with them or taking them to the park.

If we give to our children without wanting anything back except a healthy relationship, and if we love people who love our children, doesn't it seem logical that whomever created us would also want a relationship with us and would love us more if we loved his children?

Giving to Others in General

Raising children and giving to them is one way of accomplishing our purpose. But it is natural to be givers to our children, so that is not so difficult.

But how much more meaning would we get if we gave to others who *weren't* our children? It's possible that giving to others who aren't our children is a higher form of giving since it is not as easy for us. When we have to make more of an effort, that will usually bring us a higher level of personal satisfaction.

When we love others, we are giving to them. When we give to them without wanting anything back, we are fulfilling our purpose in life.

When you start fulfilling your purpose in life and give to others, you will live with tremendous energy and wake up every day excited about life. You will live with passion and a zest for life that you may have never known.

Have you ever asked yourself, "What is my purpose in life?" If you don't know, do you think it's possible to fulfill your potential? Review your daily activities and determine whether giving is a major part of your life. If not, ask yourself how you can become better at giving.

When you train yourself to give, you will be fulfilling your ultimate purpose. The more you give, the better your life will be and the more you will find out how awesome you really are.

Giving Is Living

*I profoundly feel that the art of living is the
art of giving. You're fulfilled in the moment
of giving, of doing something beyond yourself.*
—Laurance Rockefeller

Here's a story: A first-grade teacher gives each
student a balloon. She asks them to write their name
on it and put it in the hallway outside the classroom.

She then mixes up the balloons and asks the
students to go find the one with their name on it.
After about five minutes of searching, the balloons
are flying all over the place and none of the kids can
find their own.

She calls them back to the classroom, then tells
them to go grab the first balloon they see and give
it to the person whose name is on it. In less than a
minute, every child has their balloon.

The lesson: when we give to others more than
we take for ourselves, we get more. When you

become a giver, you will discover that you are more awesome and feel more awesome than you could have ever imagined.

You can give to a person, a family, or an organization. You can give money, advice, attention, or time. You can give by simply listening.

The Gift of Listening

One of my friends was going through a tough period in her life. She was in debt, having a difficult time in her marriage, and not in a good place emotionally. She was starting a new business, and she asked me for advice. I am not a business consultant, but I knew enough to give her some ideas and help her get started.

There are many classes on public speaking, but I have never seen one on how to listen. Listening is an art form. Unfortunately, many people are so focused on themselves that they are not willing or able to spend time listening to someone else.

When you truly listen, you are showing that you care, and sometimes that is all a person needs. People who are struggling and seem lost in life may just need to talk it out. Letting them do that could give them clarity.

Effective listening mostly involves simply being present and empathetic. It is no coincidence that the words "listen" and "silent" have the same letters.

All my friend needed was to have someone listen. It wasn't about my giving of money, but of my time and attention. She ultimately became a success in her business, and it all started with having someone listen to her.

Being a good listener can include providing affirmation. When one of my children comes home with an art project, usually a drawing, it is very easy for me to say, "Very nice, dear!" without making much of an effort to show that I really care. So I make sure to point out a specific part of the picture I like: "Honey, I love the way you drew the feathers on the bird." Doing this lets them know I care. Is a 5-year-old's art really important to me? Probably not, but how they feel is important.

Jack the Amazing Giver

When I started dealing in coins, I made friends with Jack, a dealer who was a few years older than I was and already a big player in the coin market. We did a lot of business together. He is one of those people you hear about and wonder if the stories are made up. With Jack, they were true. He is one of the most generous people I know, and he enjoys giving. No matter what situation he finds himself him, he gets pleasure out of giving to his friends.

We were in Las Vegas at a craps table, and one of my friends didn't have money to gamble with. Jack mentioned that he liked my friend's shirt and asked him if he wanted to sell it. My friend said sure, but he didn't have another shirt to wear in its place. Jack gave him $200 for the shirt, plus switched shirts with him. Jack probably didn't want the shirt; he was just trying to help without making him feel like he was receiving help.

Jack was a big gambler—one of those players who got everything paid for by the casino. I know because every time I was in Las Vegas for a trade show, he let me stay with him. He once stayed in the two-level suite that had been in a scene in the movie *Rain Man.* It had a giant open spiral staircase and a two-story tower of windows. It also had a TV that came out of a cabinet at the foot of the bed.

Jack would invite everyone he knew to dinner. Although he wasn't technically paying for it, this was generous; he still had to pay the tax and a hefty tip because he ordered the best food and expensive bottles of wine.

One time, Jack purchased a six-figure coin deal from me on the ski slopes at Heavenly Valley in California just so I could stay on the trip longer. I had just purchased three bags (3,000 coins) of silver dollars from the early 1880s. I needed to cut the trip short so I could process the coins and raise the money to pay for them. On the ski lift, Jack asked how much I wanted for them. I told him and he bought them on the spot! Although Jack had made a business decision to buy the coins, I had never heard of someone buying a deal this large without at least looking at the coins, especially on a ski lift! Jack only did it so I that I wouldn't cut the trip short.

Jack is generous to everyone who crosses his path, especially his friends. This fulfills his purpose in life and gives him pleasure.

Giving like this is a great start, but there are greater acts of giving.

Giving to a Stranger

A bigger act of giving would be if you did something for someone who *isn't* your family member or friend.

A musical called *Joseph and the Amazing Technicolor Dreamcoat* is based on the biblical depiction of Joseph, one of the 12 sons of Jacob. Joseph was sold into slavery by his brothers and ended up in an Egyptian jail for 12 years. While he was there, two of the pharaoh's courtiers, the wine steward and the baker, joined him.

One morning, Joseph noticed that the two courtiers looked aggrieved. He asked, "Why do you appear downcast today?" They explained that they had had dreams that they could not interpret. Joseph was able to interpret their dreams, which eventually came true after they left jail.

On the surface, you wouldn't consider this an important event in the story. But think about what jail is like. It would probably be rare for an inmate to notice another inmate's emotional state. You would think most inmates would keep to themselves and not be concerned about others. Joseph noticed that someone else was upset and decided to help. He made a decision to go out of his way and be a giver. And eventually, his gesture—offering to interpret their dreams—allowed him to get out of jail.

Years later, when the pharaoh could not interpret his own dreams, the wine steward told him that there was a man in jail who could help. The pharaoh released Joseph, who interpreted the pharaoh's dream to mean that a famine was about to descend upon Egypt. This situation became a reality, and Joseph's interpretation served as a warning that helped prevent a catastrophe.

What happened next was truly out of the ordinary: Joseph became the viceroy of Egypt! A foreigner second in command of the entire Egyptian nation was extremely out of character for a nation of Arabs. Then, because Joseph was running the country and in charge of food distribution, when his brothers came to Egypt seeking food for his family, he was able to provide it. Joseph went out of his way to give of himself, and because of it, he was able to not only get out of jail and become viceroy of Egypt but save his family from starvation.

You may never know the outcomes of your actions, but when you are a giver, your life has more meaning and purpose, and you have a stronger sense of self-worth. And when you help others fulfill their dreams, your own dreams may be more likely to come true, just like Joseph's.

As I noted in the previous chapter, parents naturally want to give to their children, but giving does not have to end when your children are grown (or if you don't have them); it can happen all the time with your family, friends, and community. You can give away money, time, effort, and emotional support.

Giving Away Money

Giving away money is not something most people do very well. Most of us need to practice it to be good at it.

Some religions, including the Christian and Muslim faiths, require that members give a percentage of their income to charitable causes. This practice started with the Bible, which stipulated that every Jew must tithe 10 percent (tithe means one-tenth) of their net income to charity. And giving away 10 percent is just the guideline for the average wage earner; if you are considered wealthy, you are expected to give 20 percent.

The reason giving money is a commandment, not just a recommendation, is that most people find it difficult. If it were easy, it wouldn't need to be a commandment.

Many people are raised to believe that the person with the most toys when they die wins. This way of thinking tends to make us hoard money, even if we have plenty. Just ask anyone worth tens of million dollars whether they think they have enough money. My guess is they will say no. No one ever thinks they have enough.

I have former colleagues who are worth tens of millions of dollars, and a few who are probably worth more than $100 million, yet they still spend many hours working to make more money. It's not that they don't enjoy the work; it's that they have not found anything more meaningful to replace the feeling of satisfaction they get from making money. It is possible that if they search a little harder, they may find something more meaningful to do with their time than continue to work. And because they are trapped in materialistic desires, being a philanthropist is not something they find appealing.

Bill and Melinda Gates, along with Warren Buffett, have pledged to give away more than half of their wealth. Warren Buffett has gone even further and said he will give away 99 percent! He realized that there is only so much you can do with money. When you reach a certain threshold, more money isn't going to significantly change your standard of living.

The difference between an upper-middle-class American and Warren Buffet is almost nominal. Aside from the fact that Buffet flies via private jet, their lives are similar in terms of standard of living.

Neither is worried about getting eaten by a wild lion or where their next meal will come from. They can both go anywhere in the world without much effort.

There is a concept from ancient teachings called Ethics of Our Fathers: "Who is rich? One who is happy with what they have." When you are never satisfied with your wealth, you will never be happy. This is why when you can find meaning in life from being a giver, you will live a much happier life.

Moses Ben Maimon (known as the Rambam), was a world-renown rabbi, physician, and astronomer in the Middle Ages, and many of his ideas still hold true. He said there are many levels of giving:

Level 9: This is the lowest form, when you give something to someone in need in a demeaning way. For example, someone comes to your door asking for money, and you make them wait, for no reason except that you are giving them something. Or you give them money but also admonish them to go out and get a job. Did you perform an act of giving even though you didn't do it with pure intentions? It's not clear.

Level 8: You are pained by the act of giving when you're asked for money, but you do not show it. One way to reduce the pain: give away a little money every day instead of giving a large sum away all at once. Using your giving muscle will train you to take pleasure in helping others and make it easier for you to give in the future.

Level 7: You cheerfully give away money when asked, but it's less than you're capable of giving. It is great that you give, but if you are making a six-figure salary and only giving away a few hundred dollars a month, you have the capacity to give more.

Level 6: You give only when you're asked. Most people give at this level. However, giving away time or money is considered more valuable when you proactively search out people or organizations that need help.

Level 5: You give away money without being asked. This is a level within everyone's capabilities. It takes practice, but when you are able to do it, you will feel awesome about yourself because you went out and made an effort to help someone.

Level 4: You give away money when you don't know the recipient but the recipient knows of you. According to the Rambam, levels 4, 3, and 2 are very high because you're donating anonymously; there are no ulterior motives. You are not doing it for the recognition of being a generous person or having something named after you or your family.

Level 3: You know the recipient of your gift, but the recipient does not know you. Everyone should try this level at least once.

Level 2: You and the recipient don't know each other.

Level 1: You give the recipient skills and the wherewithal to become self-supporting. The greatest form of giving is helping someone gain the ability to not live off of handouts. The old adage "Give a man a fish, and you will feed him for a day; show him how to catch fish, and you feed him for a lifetime" rings true.

Ask yourself a few questions and be honest about whether you are a giver. Does giving of your time or money play a part in your life? Do you give away money only when you are asked for it, or are you proactive about helping people or organizations? If you are wealthy, are you giving away enough money, or do you find it too difficult to part with large sums? When giving becomes a part of your life, you'll become awesome.

Strive to Be Your Best

*God gave you a fingerprint
that no one else has so you can
leave an imprint on someone
that no one else can.*
—Rabbi Moshe Scheiner

You are already an amazing person. The fact that you decided to pick up this book means you're serious about your personal growth. Sometimes the first step to doing anything is the hardest to achieve. You broke through that barrier by getting this far in this book. When you strive to be your best in life, you will start to blossom, and when you blossom, you'll be awesome!

Many of us struggle in different areas of our lives. We can put ourselves in a better position to overcome our challenges when we understand their origins. I like to say that every struggle we face can be summed up by an acronym (the foundation for many of my classes). It is based on our drive to be our best: **B**ody, **E**go, **S**oul, and **T**est.

Our body and soul are the main warriors on the battleground of our internal struggle. When we understand that, we can start taking steps to win the battle.

Our conflict with our ego's desire for recognition, respect, and honor is our next struggle. That involves us trying to fill the void where our self-esteem should be. Our **B**ody wants to do what feels good, our **E**go wants to do what looks good, and our **S**oul wants to do what *is* good. **T** stands for the test we have to pass every day in order to be our best.

The Body-Soul Battle

The typical body vs. soul battle starts in the morning. When your alarm wakes you up early so you can go exercise, meditate, or pray, it is *so* easy to hit the snooze button and go back to sleep. Your soul wants to wake up and hit the trail but your body wants to turn over and put its face on the coolest part of the pillow.

This is the first test of your day. Your soul knows that in the long run, you will be better off if you get out of bed, put on your running clothes, and go for a run, but your body wants immediate gratification: sleep. Your body does not care about the long-term effects of your current actions. The soul lives for the future while the body lives for whatever feels good now.

After a good run, no one says "I feel miserable," because you almost *always* feel great. No matter how hard it is to run, no matter how hot or sore you get, you feel fantastic afterward. Your soul is so happy that it blocks out anything your body is feeling. This is the same reason professional football players are able to play football outside in blizzard conditions wearing just thin jerseys. Their souls override their bodies' distaste for the freezing-cold conditions. A player is motivated because his soul overrides his body's desire to stay warm; nothing can stop him from competing.

You can make an argument that athletes are only playing for money, but I would venture that if they made 95 percent less money, most athletes would still play their sport. Why is it that 42-year-old quarterbacks will do anything to stay in the game of football, even risking devastating injury, after they have made more money than they'll ever need? A player's body would rather be sitting in a hot tub, sipping margaritas, and eating tacos with hot sauce. However, his soul wants to keep playing, and that overrides physical pain.

When your body is in control instead of your soul, you have a higher chance of abusing drugs or alcohol. How many times do people say, "I feel great!" the day after drinking heavily or doing drugs?

Probably not often, because their body is screaming about the pain they caused it and their soul wants no part of that. The soul wants to do the right thing; it does not want to be under the influence of anything that takes it away from what's good for health. When someone has been on drugs or excess amounts of alcohol for six months, you will rarely hear them say with enthusiasm, "Life is great!" At that point, life probably isn't great or they are lying to themselves.

The Temptations of Junk Food

Food addiction can be a major battle in the body-soul relationship. Think about the last time you had a plate of hot, crispy french fries staring you in the face. It's hard to resist eating *just one*. You start to rationalize that if you eat only one, you won't change anything about your health or weight, which is true. Your body wins the argument and you eat only one. Of course the fries are delicious, so you decide to eat *just one more*. Your soul is losing the battle and your body is declaring victory, crossing the finish line with a fry in each hand and two behind each ear.

Eating a french fry by itself won't do damage. What does the damage is your lack of self-control. Each time you lose self-control, it becomes easier to lose it again. That goes for having chocolate cake for dessert, especially the flourless kind that's all hot and gooey in the middle and comes with a scoop of vanilla ice cream. Try beating back your body's desires when everyone else at the table is attacking the cake with a frenzy! Your soul will likely lose that battle if your body is in charge.

This is why if you want to lose weight, it is *much* easier if you don't have any junk food in the house or anywhere around you.

Have you ever gone to the grocery store hungry and then wondered why you bought all sorts of salty, sugary, snacks? Yeah, you're not alone.

When I go to the grocery store, I eat a meal first. If you do this, you will find it is much easier to control your urges and not buy junk food.

My father always said that if you are going to eat junk food, eat ice cream. He said all snack foods, such as potato chips, pretzels, and cookies, have almost no redeeming value. Ice cream, by contrast, is full of protein, amino acids, calcium, and vitamin D. You have to love a father who tells you to go eat ice cream! I know what you may be thinking: ice cream is good for you only in moderation. Which is true, but just like with french fries, ice cream is very hard to eat in moderation.

Once I tried having a small bowl of ice cream every night. Each evening, I added a tiny bit more. What started out as a very small scoop turned into a three-scoop sundae with chocolate fudge, caramel, sprinkles, and whipped cream. By doing this, I learned that it is better for me to have ice cream only occasionally. Now, when I do it, I eat an entire half gallon, and then the urge to eat ice cream goes away for a few weeks. Of course, I am not recommending that you eat a half gallon of ice cream in one sitting (unless it's mint chocolate chip).

Back in the 1990s, getting rid of fat in food was all the rage. There was a new product called SnackWell's: a brand of cookies made with no fat. Can you imagine cookies that contained no fat? I didn't have to imagine them because when these new inventions made it to the grocery store shelves, I was waiting in line to get my hands on some. The stores were selling them as fast as they could get them in. I sat on my kitchen floor eating three packages of SnackWell's chocolate chip cookies in one sitting.

Unfortunately, what the manufacturer had done was to replace the fat with corn syrup, which is just an intensive form of sugar and extremely unhealthful. In reality, these cookies were actually worse for the body because of the sugar.

There are no shortcuts to being healthy and staying in good physical shape. The secret is simply to *eat less*. If you can train your mind to eat smaller portions, not eat between meals, and stay away from junk food, your soul will start to win the battle.

The Importance of Exercise

When it comes to losing weight, exercise is very important, although slightly less important than eating smaller portions.

Strenuous exercise makes you want to eat more often. When your body burns calories, it must replace them. People tend to rationalize that they can eat foods like cake and ice cream because "I will run it off tomorrow." That thinking works up to a certain point, but you eventually learn that *you can't outrun your fork!*

When you are young, you can get away with working off all the calories from a poor diet. As most people get older, they exercise less or less vigorously, but the pace at which the fork goes into their mouth doesn't decrease. Eating unhealthy foods and overeating will eventually catch up with you. This is why it pays to listen to your soul instead of your body when making food choices.

Overeating is a major cause of weight gain. A contributing factor is that there is a lag time between when your stomach is full and when your brain registers that your stomach is full. More than a thousand years ago, the Rambam wrote that people should stop eating when they are 75 percent full. The body-soul dilemma was an issue even then, although people didn't have to deal with SnackWell's.

When I started traveling for business in my early 20s, I was surprised by how much food people would eat. When I went to a restaurant, I was always looking for ways to save money. I would either just eat an appetizer or try to split a main course with someone. Most of my dining companions would order an appetizer, a main dish, and a dessert. I was full just from the appetizer! It wasn't surprising that over the years, many people in my industry became severely overweight.

When you start living by listening to your soul instead of your body, you will realize that you can live on fewer calories.

Do you eat mindlessly? This is when you are reading a book, watching TV, or having a conversation while stuffing chips, peanuts, popcorn, or some other snack in your mouth. It's mindless because you're not eating because you're hungry; you're eating because the food is there. How can you enjoy food if your mind is preoccupied?

If you have children and they see you eating mindlessly, they will likely do it, too. Then, possibly later in life, you will wonder why your children are overweight. They watched what you did and followed in your footsteps. So put down those Pringles!

Thinking for Yourself

Be careful about what you hear about food choices. Have you ever been on a fad diet and then, years later, realized that it was unhealthy?

For instance, do you remember the Atkins diet? I know what was going through people's minds when they heard about it: "I can eat all the steak, bacon, cheese, and eggs I want, as long as I stay away from vegetables? Count me in!"

I knew people on that diet. I would see them during breakfast at a hotel, ordering an enormous five-egg omelet loaded with cheese and enough bacon to cover their entire plate. I *knew* that wasn't going to work out so well!

If you don't think something makes sense in terms of nutrition, it probably doesn't. It's always a good idea to filter the information you hear or read and extract what's true for you.

Today there is much debate about science. On social media, many people state with certainty that science is real. I love science and the discoveries we can learn from it. I believe that scientific facts are correct until they're proven incorrect, which some are, such as when we find out years later that a research finding was flawed or misconstrued.

What you should be looking for in science is unbiased truth.

You may hear someone say a certain area of town is safe. All it takes is a few reports of robberies, muggings, or carjackings, and suddenly it's unsafe. Just as a part of town is considered safe until it becomes infiltrated with crime, facts are only true until there is new scientific evidence to refute them. You need to think for yourself! OK, back to our regularly scheduled programming.

Stay Away from Sugar and Carbs

The more carbs and sugar you eat, the hungrier you'll feel later. I don't mean just hungry, I mean *famished!* You'll feel like you are starving. Consuming foods high in sugar and starch any time of the day causes a spike in blood sugar. Your pancreas releases a hormone called insulin, which tells your cells to absorb more blood sugar, causing your blood-sugar level to drop.

Your soul will lose the battle with your body when you have intense hunger pangs. I hate to even call it a battle because it would be like Mike Tyson fighting Pee-Wee Herman. Your soul can't win that battle just as Pee-Wee can't outbox Mike Tyson. The lower insulin level turns you into an animal (I'm not saying Mike Tyson is an animal, but he *did* bite someone's ear off, twice!). You then want to eat the first thing you see without considering its health benefits. This is why at 11 a.m., the drive-through line at McDonald's is around the corner of the building and the line at the salad bar restaurant doesn't start getting long until 1 p.m. It's because people who eat healthfully don't have spikes in their blood sugar that make them ravenous, so they can wait longer to eat lunch.

I used to eat a bagel for breakfast every morning, and by mid-morning, I felt like I was starving. I would have eaten my cat if I could have caught her. (OK, I would not have eaten *my* cat, but I would have eaten my neighbor's.)

I would then eat the thing I could most quickly get my hands on, which was usually a candy bar or bag of chips. How healthful was my day going to be? Not very.

To help your soul win the battle with your body, eat protein in the morning. The hunger pangs you may get after eating protein are considerably less intense than the ones you may have after eating sugar and carbs. You will notice that you don't have the same hunger pangs later in the morning. You will be able to last until lunchtime, when you can make better food choices.

The same idea holds true when you are planning to fast. Dr. Google provides significant evidence that it is healthy to periodically fast a number of times a year. I fast for six days a year (for spiritual reasons). Fasting promotes blood-sugar control, reduces inflammation, boosts brain function and metabolism, may delay aging and cancer growth, and provides many more health benefits. If you eat a meal high in protein with no carbs or sugar before you fast, you will find that it is significantly easier for you to make it through the entire day of fasting.

Recently I have been eating salads for both breakfast and lunch, with fish or cheese as the protein, and then for dinner, I eat whatever I want. Do I miss my bagel? Of course. As my reward for eating protein and salad the rest of the week, I have a bagel for lunch on Friday. I am much more in control of my body, and my body's cravings are not controlling me. If I happen to get hungry in the late morning, I eat a piece of fruit, and I can then make it to lunchtime. You will never see me sitting in the drive-through line at a fast-food joint, about to eat my steering wheel… or a cat!

A number of years ago, I started following a kosher diet. It helped me put my soul in charge of my body. Some people questioned why I would limit what I eat. Some said I had made myself a slave to my diet. It is really the opposite. I was making a choice about what goes in my mouth. I was not giving in to my cravings. I am not a slave to my desires; I am the master of them.

All kosher animals are passive and docile, not aggressive predators. There is a saying that "You are what you eat." If that's true, and you eat aggressive animals, it could theoretically cause you to become aggressive. This could cause your body to take control of your soul. At this point, you are losing the body vs. soul battle. What you should be striving for is having your soul be in charge of your body. That is the ultimate in being able to be your best.

The Ego's Desire for Respect

Your body wants to do what feels good, your soul wants to do what is good, and your ego likes to do what makes you look good. The need to fulfill your ego comes from the need to build your self-esteem.

Genuine self-esteem comes from within yourself, not from looking to others for respect. Relying on others for approval can make you feel hollow and insecure.

Genuine self-respect comes from doing good, not looking good. The body is happy with the feeling of being important, in any way it can, but the soul looks for what's *truly* important. You can focus on what's truly important by focusing on attaining accomplishment and meaning in your life.

People with healthy egos don't blame others when things don't go their way. They don't make excuses for every failure in their life. They take responsibility for themselves. They tend to learn from failures, get right back up on their feet, and not make the same mistakes.

Your ego's desire for respect may manifest itself in the type of car you drive, the size of your house, and the titles you strive for at work. You may want others to see you as successful, wealthy, attractive, smart, funny, powerful, and a host of other characteristics that will boost your ego.

Unless you are continually hosting huge parties, why would a family of four need a 12,000 square-foot house?

It's the same with expensive cars. There is really one purpose for a car: to get from point A to point B. A Honda would do it just as well, more reliably, and for much less money. There has been so much technological advancement in automobile safety and features that the only reason to buy a $100,000 car would be to satisfy your ego. You can have a beautiful car with all the bells and whistles for less than half the price of some high-end cars.

I had this dream that when I could afford a Porsche, I would buy one. However, after I bought one, I realized that the best part about owning it had been the *anticipation* of owning it. When I was able to acquire it, I did not feel a need to have something so extravagant.

A Porsche can hit speeds as high as 200 miles per hour. Unless you like taking your car to a racetrack or driving recklessly, why does a car need to go that fast? Because car makers know it will fulfill people's desires and they will sell more cars.

I bought the Porsche not because I really wanted it. I felt the pull of societal pressure. When I became successful, I believed that I needed to show off the fact that I had succeeded financially.

Did I enjoy owning this fancy car? Yes, for about two months. Then it became a liability for a number of reasons. The main reason I sold it was that owning it was not as fulfilling as I thought it would be. It was a case of my ego thinking I needed to prove my success, when in reality, my soul was figuring out that materialism wasn't going to make me happy.

There is another way to know whether your ego is controlling your decision making: if you seek a leadership position just for the attention and to build your resume and social standing. There are many prestigious board positions with both non-profit and public companies. Ask yourself whether you want to do it for the prestige or you sincerely want to help. What's motivating you? Step up if you are needed, but be content to sit on the sidelines if you aren't.

Someone who is awesome does not need to be given accolades and credit. They are happy to take pleasure in what they have accomplished. They are happy to thank others for even the smallest bit of help. They don't have to brag about their achievements or show off how much money they make by having an extravagant house or car. They would rather use their money to help people in need. They do not need people to tell them they are important; they *are* important.

Be Nice to People

A lack of self-esteem may show itself in the way someone treats people they feel are "below their pay grade," such as those in the service industry. People with low self-esteem subconsciously try to bring others down because they feel like it raises them up and makes them feel better about themselves.

A great way to determine whether someone has a damaged ego is to observe how they treat people in the service industry. Have you ever been in a restaurant and seen someone be abusive to a waiter? I was embarrassed while eating out because a friend would complain to the server about a spot on a glass or a dirty utensil, or say the dish he ordered was not what he expected. He was complaining to show his power; his ego was trying to compensate for his low self-esteem. You can forgive someone if this happens occasionally, but when it happens consistently, the person has some serious issues. The last time this happened, I told my friend I would never eat in a restaurant with him again.

I teach my children that they should be nice to *everyone.* It does not matter if it is a maid, a gardener, or a waiter; be nice to everyone, especially those who are doing things for you.

Let Go of Difficult People

Some people are just difficult, and you may come to resent them for the way they treat you. How do you deal with them?

If someone is not nice to you and that bothers you, you are allowing them to get into your head. I always say, "Don't let other people ruin your day."

My wife reminds me of an analogy when my ego gets bruised by something that someone does or says to me. She says to stop holding it in and let it go.

When you hold in resentment, it's as if you are renting space in your head to these people for free. Holding it in just causes you to be tormented. When you look at it from that perspective, you may be more likely to let it go.

Try holding a cup of water in the palm of your hand and extending your arm out in front of you. After just a few minutes, your arm starts to feel a little uncomfortable. After half an hour, it gets *very* uncomfortable. Hold it there for an hour and your arm will be in excruciating pain.

That is what you are doing to yourself when you are holding in resentment toward someone. You are causing yourself pain by not letting it go.

How do you improve your emotions by not letting things fester in your head? How can you live with a healthy ego that is not easily bruised and doesn't need accolades?

Always Judge People Favorably

Judging people favorably means that whenever someone does something you don't like, you don't take it personally. You may feel like they are doing it on purpose, but most people really want to be good; they just can't help acting that way. They may have come from a dysfunctional family or have enormous insecurities. Judging people favorably is a great way to live a much more happy and awesome life. Always judge others in the way you would want them to judge you.

The best way to release the stress of dealing with a difficult person is to feel sorry for them. Someone who behaves inappropriately is dealing with a lot more emotional baggage than what you may be carrying.

Be grateful that you are not going through what they are. They could also make a positive change and turn into an amazing person later in their life.

Another way to deal with difficult people is to imagine that everyone you meet is a 50-chapter book. What you are experiencing with someone is just one chapter. They may be in Chapter 25 of their life, and you have no idea what happened in the first 24 chapters. They may have gone through emotional trauma and they are projecting their pain onto you. You may be lacking crucial information on why they are acting that way. Remembering this will help you keep your temper and condemnation in check. You have no idea what the last chapters of their book will look like. They may turn out to be amazing and kind!

All people have positive qualities; these may just be buried beneath confusion and pain. If you make an effort, you can see the beauty in everyone. (*48 Ways to Wisdom,* Coopersmith & Simmons)

Judging people favorably is a great way to live without resentment or the need to boost your ego.

Choosing Your Soul over Your Body

Your soul wants what's best for your body. Your soul makes choices that can benefit you decades later. Your soul does not live for immediate gratification. When you can make decisions based on what your soul wants, you can be happier and healthier, and have better relationships.

I like to say that soul stands for **S**haring **O**ur **U**nlimited **L**ove. We can share our love with others, but we must also love ourselves.

When you love someone, you do only things that are good for them; you treat them positively.

If you love your children, you don't serve them potato chips for every meal and allow them to watch TV all day. Will your children like those choices? They would probably prefer to eat junk food and sit on the couch. You limit the amount of junk food they eat and the amount of TV they watch because you love them.

When you love yourself, you make healthy decisions for yourself.

If you love yourself, you are less likely to eat that french fry, gooey piece of chocolate cake, or bowl of mint-chocolate-chip ice cream (OK, maybe not the ice cream). If you love yourself, you know that getting out of bed may be a struggle, but you look forward to the feeling of finishing a run, completing a yoga class, or reciting a prayer. Knowing that something is good for you helps your soul win the battle with your body.

Making choices based on your soul's desires instead of your body's will have long-lasting effects that you may not immediately recognize. It is the same dilemma as when you're eating a french fry or struggling with anything. Eating one fry won't hurt you, a single three-mile run won't make you healthier, and eating one carrot won't give you enough vitamins to improve your vision. However, when you train yourself to choose your soul over your body in small daily decisions, it will help you make a positive difference in the long run. You're willing to forgo immediate physical gratification for the long-term pleasure your soul desires.

The Test You Take Every Day

T stands for the test you struggle with between your body, ego, and soul.

It's hard to pass a test that you don't know is being given, so the first thing you must do is recognize that there is a test going on. If you are not aware of it, you will not be able to engage in it.

Think about what part of you is in charge of making the choices in your life. Is your soul in charge? Are you listening only to what your body wants? Which part would you prefer to listen to? When you can understand which desires are in control, you have an opportunity to overcome them and live the life you want.

If you struggle with any of the issues mentioned earlier, you are being tested. When you become aware that you're being tested, you can choose to start making decisions that are good for your soul. Imagine not having to struggle to turn down that piece of cake or french fry. Imagine being able to wake up every morning motivated to start your day with prayer, meditation, or a run. When you get to the point where your soul is in charge of your body, you will understand what it means to be your best.

Change Your Perceptions

*Miracles happen every day,
change your perception of what a miracle is
and you'll see them all around you.*
—Jon Bon Jovi

There is a joke about a woman who has a pet duck:

One day she notices that the duck
is unresponsive, so she takes it to
the vet.

The vet looks at the duck, looks at
the woman, and says, "Lady, your duck
is dead."

She responds, "My duck isn't dead!"

The vet answers, "Lady, your duck
is dead!"

She responds, "I want more tests!"

The vet rolls his eyes and says, "OK, I'll order more tests."

The vet leaves the room and a Labrador Retriever walks through the door. It walks over to the duck, jumps up, and puts its front paws on the table. It sniffs the duck, looks at the woman with a sad face, shakes its head, and walks out of the room.

A minute later, a cat walks into the room. It jumps on the table, sniffs the duck, looks at the woman with a sad face, shakes its head, and says, "Meow." It jumps down and walks out.

The vet walks in and says, "The results came back, and I'm sorry to tell you the tests confirm that your duck is definitely dead."

The woman responds, "I know, I know, just give me the bill."

The doctor hands her the bill and she says, "$180 just to tell me my duck is dead?"

The vet responds, "Lady, normally I charge $20, but you asked for a lab report and a cat scan, and those are extra."

Sometimes what should be obvious isn't obvious.

If you're reading this book, you are awesome, but it may not be obvious to you.

My goal is to help you change your perceptions so that you clearly know it. You received amazing gifts at birth, and you have everything you need to be great, yet you may fail to realize how awesome your potential is. You may be taking things for granted.

There are a number of ways to change your perceptions. One is to change how you believe others perceive you. One is to change how you perceive yourself. The last is to change how you perceive the world.

The Power of a Smile:
How Others Perceive You

How many times a day do you see your face? If you're a guy like me, maybe at the most, three. Yet, if you come to my class or we work together, how often do I see your face? All day. Which means you really don't own your face. Even though it's yours, I have to live with it staring at me much more than you do.

How you show your reactions affects me and everyone around you. If you smile, you make everyone else smile. If you scowl, everyone around you is affected negatively. If you want to become genuinely happy, start being someone who likes being around people. Do it for yourself even though it is helping everyone else.

If you smile, even when you're having a bad day, not only will you feel better about yourself, but you can change how others perceive you. "Fake it until you make it:" pretend to put on a happy face even if you aren't happy. Your smile will positively affect others, which, in turn, will come back to you. If you make people smile, you will smile more. You may think this seems foolish and maybe even fraudulent, but you are putting yourself and everyone around you in a good mood. You can stay upset or angry at someone and have a scowl on your face, but that isn't going to make you feel better. It's better to put a smile on your face, see how it can positively affect others, and see how you feel better.

Dress for Success

Think about when you wore a tuxedo or formal dress to a wedding. You walked taller, spoke in a more positive tone, and felt good about yourself. This positive feeling affected how others perceived you.

How you dress affects how others perceive you and influences how you act.

How you dress is related to your confidence level when you talk. The best salespeople in the world (including those doing telephone sales, so their clients can't see them), generally dress impeccably. It makes a difference.

"Casual Friday" is popular in the business world. Don't buy into it! That will take you down the path of mediocrity, even if it's only one day a week. (Soon we will hear about Messy Monday, T-shirt Tuesday, Wacky Wednesday, and Thoughtless Thursday.) I can guarantee you that many people who feel awesome about themselves—the ones who are at the top of their games—may not be into Casual Friday (or any casual-dress day).

If you want to be successful in life—not only looking successful but actually achieving success—dress the part.

How You Perceive Yourself: You Are the Most Valuable Thing in the World

If you could look at yourself as you would look at a highly advanced machine, such as the F-35 joint strike fighter jet, you might see yourself in a different light. We marvel at technological advancements such as jets and smartphones, but we may not think of ourselves as infinitely more advanced than anything humanity has been able to produce. Looking at yourself differently may change your perception of yourself.

Imagine that someone offers you a billion dollars for your eyesight. Would you sell your eyes? Probably not. (OK, I know you are being a smart aleck and saying you would, but there is *no way* you would do it). An offer like this would mean you are worth more than a billion dollars for your eyes alone. If that were the case, think about how much everything else in your body would be worth. If someone were blind, either from birth or after having an accident, and suddenly there was a life-saving procedure that could let them see again, they would probably stop at nothing to get that operation. How would that person feel after getting their vision back? Amazing. So in this situation, if you have two eyes, you would be jumping for joy, excited about how much value you have just in your eyes, and you would realize that you have been given the greatest gift in the world.

Understanding Levels of Gratitude

How can you change your perceptions and realize how awesome you are? You must have gratitude. Why do you need gratitude in order to change your perceptions? Someone who is truly thankful appreciates everything they have.

I know what you're thinking: "I have gratitude; I'm thankful for my eyes." That's a good start, but you need a deeper understanding of what it means to live with the *highest* level of gratitude or you won't get to being awesome.

Gratitude is a feeling of appreciation toward someone or about something. If a friend takes you out for a nice dinner, you express your gratitude by thanking them. If your boss gives you a raise, you show gratitude by saying thank you. If you win the lottery, you feel grateful for the money you won.

This is one level of having gratitude, but there is a higher level, just as there are many levels of being happy: cheerful, elated, delighted, ecstatic. Which level of happiness would you choose? I would choose ecstatic.

Understanding and living with the highest level of gratitude will take you all the way to awesome.

This higher level of gratitude is when you know *whom* you are thanking in every situation, even in a situation in which there is no one to thank. If you were driving down the highway and another car lost control and swerved, missing you by a few inches, and then crashed into the guardrail, what would you say to yourself? You would certainly have gratitude for not being involved in a crash. You might say you were lucky or exclaim "Thank goodness!"

When you say "Thank goodness," what do you mean? To whom are you grateful? Whom or what is goodness? Does your local DMV have a Thank Goodness department you can call to show your appreciation? Is there a Thank Goodness app?

In my days of buying and selling rare coins, I would sometimes make a counteroffer on the price the seller wanted to charge for a coin. Occasionally I would hear from the seller, "I'll sell it to you at your price because it's good karma."

What's karma? It's the concept that every negative thought or action we think or do will come back to hurt us, and every positive thought or action we think or do will come back as something good. That certainly doesn't sound random. In fact, it sounds *far* from random. If someone were to say that to me, I would ask, "Who is in charge of karma and how can I get some more of it?"

In physics, Newton's third law states that for every action, there is an equal and opposite reaction. That makes sense in the physical world. Although doing a good deed for someone is a physical action, the credit for doing the good deed isn't physical. If a physical action gets a physical reaction, then the credit for the good deed would be a different kind of reaction. Let's call it a spiritual reaction.

For example, if you help someone move furniture, the good feeling or "credit" you get from being the giver isn't physical, it's spiritual. So if doing something good for someone causes a spiritual action, there would have to be a spiritual reaction. Maybe karma is the spiritual reaction you get for doing something good for someone?

I don't think Newton's third law has anything to do with a spiritual reaction. So who is in charge of karma? Who is in charge of spiritual reactions? Is there a karma app similar to the Thank Goodness app?

In 2004, the third-largest earthquake ever recorded, a 9.0 on the Richter scale, caused a tsunami that killed hundreds of thousands of people in Indonesia. The news reports referred to Mother

Nature unleashing her fury. When Mother Nature is blamed, to whom are they referring?

Barely avoiding a serious accident and surviving a disaster are situations in which you would feel thankful to have survived. You would certainly be living with gratitude.

Know Whom You're Thanking

As I said in Secret #6, either everything is random or it's not. If someone does something good for you, that act isn't a random occurrence, and there is someone you should be thanking. If something good happens to you through a random occurrence and you feel grateful for that random event, how much value would your gratitude have? Probably not as much. Why? You would be thankful to a random situation, which means no one had control over it. What do you think would equate with a higher level of gratitude: thanking someone or thanking a random circumstance? From my perspective, when you can thank someone, you are living with a much higher level of gratitude than when you can thank a random occurrence.

Do you want to live knowing you're awesome? Do you want to live with the clarity that when you credit karma, thank goodness, or cite Mother Nature, you're comfortable believing that they are all part of one energy source that scientists say created everything in the universe, including you?

Having gratitude means thanking the Creator who put you on Earth and gave you all the ingredients you need to thrive. That's the highest level of gratitude, and that's living awesomely.

The Magic of a Special Gift

Imagine that you're a big fan of Barbra Streisand. She is coming to town to sing at a gala for your favorite charitable organization.

When you arrive at the event, you see officials shaking hands with her, followed by a long line of people. As you wait to shake the hand of Barbra Streisand, your excitement increases with each step closer you get to being face to face with her.

You shake her hand. She holds it. She doesn't let it go like she did with everyone else. She says "I love your earrings." You think to yourself, did Barbra just say something to me? Am I in a dream?

You say "Thank you." Not knowing what to say and being completely flustered, you respond "And I love yours." You continue your conversation for a minute or two.

She asks you your table number so she can come over and talk to you. After you sit down, she sits in the empty chair next to you. After 45 minutes of chatting, she leaves to put on her performance. She then comes over and says goodbye to you.

You just had the night of your life!

It's now six months later and your husband is going to take you out for your birthday. A few hours before you leave, a package is delivered. Inside is a beautiful pink cashmere sweater. You open the card and it says, "Happy Birthday from Barbra Streisand." You scream and almost faint. You can't believe Barbra remembered your birthday!

You put on the sweater. That evening, everywhere you go, people make comments about how beautiful it is. You answer: "Barbra Streisand gave it to me for my birthday!" You don't really answer, it's more like screaming with excitement.

You are having one of the most memorable and exciting nights of your life…except, it isn't happening.

What's really happening is that your husband is taking you out for your birthday. It's a cold night, so you look for a sweater in your closet and you find a beautiful pink cashmere one. You can't remember where it came from. Regardless, it is gorgeous and perfect to wear on your birthday. Everywhere you go, you get complements on it.

The only difference is in how you respond. You comment that you are not sure where it came from and that you think someone left it in your closet.

Both stories and both sweaters are *exactly* the same except for one detail. One sweater was given to you by Barbra and you found the other in your closet and don't remember where it came from.

Which would you rather wear?

Most people would choose the one from Barbra. Why? You know she gave you it! Wearing something that someone gave you, especially someone you love, is much more meaningful.

Why can't you have the same amount of joy from wearing a sweater you found in your closet? Because you have no idea where it came from. That's it! That's the only difference between your having a nice night on the town and an *awesome* night on the town.

Can you imagine if you could live your whole life knowing where everything came from?

I'm writing this book to help you live knowing that you're awesome and that you can have an amazing life.

If you could receive so much joy from wearing a sweater, think about how much more you could get by realizing that your eyes, heart, brain, looks, talents, skills, personality, and everything you need in order to function are gifts from the Creator who loves you. All you have to do is change your perceptions in life and know that everything you have is not random, but a gift. When you have gratitude for that gift, you'll enjoy it so much more.

Learning about Gratitude

One of the first things my wife and I teach our kids when they're little is to say thank you. Why do we feel that it is so valuable for them to learn that? Does it really make a difference if your kid doesn't say thank you when you give them a cookie? Does your day change if you don't get a thank you? Probably not. But you are trying to teach them to have gratitude and say thank you for their own benefit.

What does it matter if your kids are grateful? Because when *you* know when *you* are grateful, you enjoy what you're grateful for so much more. You are teaching your children to enjoy what life has to offer and not take it for granted. You are teaching them that when they say thank you, they will get much more pleasure from the cookie.

Learning to show gratitude is a skill that we must work on daily. How can we do it? And how can parents teach it to their children?

Earlier, I discussed expressing gratitude to people and organizations that have helped you. I noted that there are situations in which there is no one to show gratitude toward. You may attribute it to goodness, karma, Mother Nature, or luck. In those cases, it's hard to show the highest level of gratitude because you're not thanking anyone. You may have gratitude, but it isn't gratitude that will get you to awesome.

When something good happens to you and there is no one to thank, thank the Creator. When you're walking down the street and drop your cell phone and see that it isn't broken, thank the Creator. When you're driving down the street and you miss hitting an animal, thank the Creator.

When you are able to do that, you will be living with a lot more clarity. If you are not able to say that, continue saying "Thank goodness" or whatever it is you say, but keep in mind that deep down, your soul *wants* to thanks the Creator but you are just not real with it yet. You will eventually be able to say it.

The Creator of the world loves you and wants you to be great and knows that you are awesome. You should know it, too. Showing gratitude to *someone,* especially someone that created you, is a very important key to realizing how awesome you are.

How You Perceive the World

One of my mentors taught me that some people "leave their mind so open that their brains fall out." They stop thinking for themselves and base their opinions only on what their friends and family think, or they simply parrot the most popular opinions in society. Their opinions may indicate a warped sense of reality.

When a Nazi officer in the German army woke up in the morning, he didn't think of himself as going out to murder innocent people. A dictator doesn't think his heavy-handed form of ruling is unfair. A murderer doesn't think what they did was wrong. In all of these examples, the person justifies unthinkable actions because their perceptions of the world are distorted.

Getting to awesome means perceiving the world in an unbiased, rational way. Much of what we hear in the media is biased and may not be objectively true. One media source says the president is the most evil person based on something he's done, and another praises him for doing the exact same thing. We have to dissect everything to get to the truth.

A similar thing happens when someone tells me they are getting divorced. They tell me why their spouse is horrible, and I don't quite believe everything they tell me. If you listen to the husband, it's her fault. If you listen to the wife, it's his fault. What's the truth? It's usually somewhere in the middle.

When someone is awesome, they realize that they must initially take everything they hear with a grain of salt. They have the ability to decipher what is objectively true and what is false.

Due to our biases, we may fail to see the truth, and, as a result, we miss amazing opportunities and relationships.

I once stumbled on an opportunity that almost no one else saw: I discovered possibly one of the most valuable coins in the world. Almost every other coin dealer and collector had seen the same coin, but due to their inherent biases, they had not identified its true value.

The 1921 Saint-Gaudens $20 Gold Coin

In August 2006, I was closely studying the coins to be sold at a major auction in Denver. When I saw one of the highlights, a 1921 Saint-Gaudens $20 gold coin, my mouth dropped open. I was shocked not because I was looking at a very valuable coin (worth about $200,000) but because it was not a general-circulation coin, which was how the certification company and auction company had classified it.

What I was looking at was a proof. Proof coins are special coins made for collectors, and they are highly desirable. They are struck with a polished die that gives them a mirrored look. Saint-Gaudens $20 gold coin proofs were made only from 1907–1915. However, I seemed to be looking at a proof coin from 1921. Not only was this an extremely rare coin, it was not supposed to exist as a proof! It was not listed in any record books or price guides (it is now).

Imagine what I must have felt when I looked at this coin and could easily tell that it was a proof (my legs were *really* shaking).

Because it was so obvious to me, I figured that a number of other dealers had realized the same thing.

My first thought was "What is this coin worth?" Gold collectors pay big bucks for rare gold coins— into the millions of dollars. My first thought was that it was worth at least a few million, but that didn't seem like enough for a highly prized, unique coin in one of the most popular series of U.S. coins. Based on the valuations of other rare coins sold in the past, I started to think it could be worth much more than $5 million!

Since this coin was previously unknown and I didn't have the means to pay anything near what I thought it was worth, I decided to bid up to $1.5 million, expecting that I would not have to pay anywhere near that price. After all, based on its current grade, it was listed as a $200,000 coin. I knew that between my credit line with the auction company and my bank credit line, I could stretch to $1.5 million. I was thinking that if I had the money, I would be bidding upward of at least a few million dollars. That's how strongly I believed in what I had discovered.

This is where it got really interesting.

I knew a dealer in the business who had the ability to correctly identify this coin *and* the gumption to make every attempt to buy it. He was extremely tough competition, and when he wants to buy a coin, it is very difficult to try to outbid him. I had a dilemma on my hands. It wasn't like a few thousand dollars were at stake. This was potentially millions of dollars. If he discovered the coin, he would either bid it up and cost me a lot of money in the process or buy it himself.

I considered proposing to him that we partner on the deal. However, if you take on a partner, lots of things can go wrong. It is common for partnerships to turn sour. My father always taught me to avoid doing that. He said if you *have* to go into a partnership, make sure the other person has more money than you. This other dealer didn't have more money. Plus, if he *didn't* happen to realize the true value of the coin, I didn't want to tip him off.

After much deliberation, I decided to call his cell phone number. If he answered, I would present him with an offer to split it with me, and if he didn't, I would try to buy it on my own. I was only going to call once.

I called him and there was no answer.

That unanswered call cost me $1.3M because he also figured out what the coin was worth and bid it up *way* past his limit. I ended up buying it for my maximum limit.

I paid $1.5M for a coin that could have sold for less than $200,000. The amazing thing was that no one else had figured out it was a proof. Some people knew it looked different, but they didn't realize it was a proof. Why? Because in their minds, it could not have existed. There were no records of the United States Mint making proofs for any denomination of coin that year!

Sometimes the obvious isn't obvious. When you are able to change your perceptions of yourself, other people, and everything in the world, you can open yourself up to amazing possibilities.

When you believe in something, even if it goes against what everyone else is saying, you better have strong convictions. It took a few years for the coin-business establishment to accept that the 1921 Saint-Gaudens gold coin was a proof.

Many years later, I ended up selling this coin to my underbidder for a considerable profit. He is very patient and realizes that it will eventually sell for a world-record price. It would not surprise me if it sold for more than $10M someday.

But again, the interesting point is that virtually none of the experts in the coin business identified the actual value of this coin. Even after the auction, when they became aware of the circumstances, some of them still didn't believe that it could be that valuable. I think that because they believed proofs hadn't been made in 1921, they were unable to connect the dots.

I pride myself on believing that people are good and on always seeing their positive traits. I applied that character trait to evaluating coins. I do not let previous ideas, concepts, or perceptions cloud my vision in terms of what a coin could be worth.

Changing my perceptions and being able to see past the obvious certainly helped me. It can also help you. Make it a habit to remember that there is hidden treasure everywhere; you just have to open your eyes and see it. There is more to the world than meets your eye. This will lead you toward becoming awesome.

- If you want to be awesome, ask yourself some serious questions:
- Are you stuck in your ways of thinking?
- Are great opportunities passing you by because you aren't willing to change your views?
- Are you living with the highest level of gratitude?
- Whom are you thanking in a situation in which there's no one to thank?

In the parable about the duck, it wasn't obvious to the woman that her duck was dead. It wasn't obvious to the coin experts that they were staring at possibly the most valuable coin in the world. If you can change your perceptions, you will discover things about yourself and the world that you didn't know existed.

Be real about who you are thanking and put a smile on your face. Always show gratitude, and if there is no obvious recipient, thank the Creator. When you are able to live with the highest level of gratitude, you will live every day as though you're wearing Barbra Streisand's sweater, and it doesn't get any better than that.

Your Journey Is Your Endgame

*It is impossible to live without failing
at something, unless you live so cautiously
that you might as well not have lived at all,
in which case you have failed by default.*
—J.K. Rowling

When you are near the end of your life, will you look back and be satisfied with everything you accomplished? Not many of us will be able to do that.

There is one way you can be sure you'll end your life satisfied and content: realize that every part of your life, the good and the bad, the happy and the sad, the exciting and the tedious, is all part of your journey.

Most people live their lives thinking *If I do this, I'll get that.* When you have a project, mission, or goal you are focused on, crossing the finish line is the way you determine success.

To discover how awesome you are, you have to look back with the mindset that everything you attempted in your life has been successful, even your failures. The final goal is not the endgame; it's the *journey itself.*

You work hard to make money so you can afford to buy a nice house. You exercise to stay healthy and in shape. You study to achieve good grades. You take the bar exam to be able to practice law. You train long hours in a sport so you can qualify for a league or even the Olympics. If you do this, you get that.

However, when you live life with the mindset of *Do this, get that,* you're missing out on the whole purpose of a meaningful life. You can enjoy life more with a *Do this, live that* mentality. Living life for the journey will bring you much more pleasure because it doesn't matter if you get to the endgame. When you realize this, you'll find out that you are really awesome.

Living without Fear

Can you imagine if you had no fear of trying anything in life? Fear is what keeps us from getting out of our comfort zones and taking risks. Fear keeps us from attempting to open a new business, growing as an individual, allowing ourselves to be who we're capable of becoming. When you know that the journey is your endgame, you may feel less afraid and be willing to take more risks.

There is a saying that the path to greatness is lined with the stepping stones of failure. Fear of failure is actually fear of success, because failure is *part of* success.

When Thomas Edison was asked about the key ingredient that allowed him to invent the light bulb, he answered that he first had to find 10,000 ways to *fail* at making a light bulb. Every step he took and every failure he had while inventing the light bulb was part of his journey.

Your Life's Puzzle

Imagine that your life is a giant jigsaw puzzle. Everything you do while you are alive brings you one piece closer to completing the puzzle. You want to look back and see how ornate, beautiful, and intricate your puzzle is so that you can take pleasure in what you've accomplished. You want your life to have been as meaningful and fulfilling as possible, but that does not mean it will have been easy. The more complex your puzzle, the more pleasure you will have putting the puzzle together.

What happens when you finish a real jigsaw puzzle? You feel good about your accomplishment for about 3 seconds, then you start to think about the *next* puzzle you want to put together. So why go through all the aggravation of doing a puzzle if the satisfaction will only last a short time? The pleasure of doing a puzzle lies in the assembly of it, piece by piece. The joy you get comes from the flexing of your brain muscles to figure out how the pieces fit together. The real joy isn't in finishing the puzzle, it's in the experience of putting it together.

There is a story about a man who wants to hike to the top of a mountain. As he is walking up the trail, he sees a pilot standing next to a helicopter. The pilot asks, "Where are you going?" He responds, "To the top of the mountain." The pilot asks, "Would you like me to take you there"? The hiker thinks about it for a second, then politely says, "No, thank you." The pilot says, "I thought you wanted to get to the top of the mountain?" The hiker responds, "I do, but I want to hike up the mountain myself."

This is a nice way to think about life. We think we're on a journey to try to accomplish something we assume will bring us meaning, when in reality, we can find meaning and pleasure in the journey itself.

We think that once we achieve what we're after, once we reach our endgame, once we succeed in reaching our goal, *then* everything will be great, and if we don't, we will have failed. A marathon runner may train for many years to get to the Olympics but never make the team. An inventor may work diligently to develop a new product but never get a patent. A painter may work for years on a masterpiece that no one ever purchases. Did these people fail? Certainly not.

When we look back at our lives, we will realize that the journey was the endgame.

It may not be until later that you discover that every piece in your life's puzzle helps make it a beautiful, complex design. Many of those pieces may have been difficult to put together, and at the time, you couldn't fathom how they would have fit in your puzzle. You may not have understood why difficult experiences happened to you. It may have been hard to contemplate why you lost someone close to you, why you got a deadly diagnosis, why you got into a horrific accident, why you couldn't find your soulmate, why you couldn't pay your bills. Every piece *does* belong in your puzzle, even if it seems like it might not.

When I look back at my life so far, every experience, each achievement and challenge, was just one puzzle piece, waiting to be added to create one unique, beautiful design. This is something you don't realize while it is happening. It's only when you are much older that you understand that everything that's happened to you has not only been part of your journey, but something from which you could learn and grow.

There is a saying that youth is wasted on the young because when you are young, you haven't developed the ability to look at challenges as opportunities for personal growth. If you are able to go through life without any challenges, then you have a great life, but you never have a chance to see how challenges would have shaped you. Never having to struggle will have made your puzzle pieces fit together much more easily, but your design will not be as intricate.

The Puzzle Pieces of My Life

I grew up in nice neighborhood in suburban Northern Virginia. I was raised in a loving home where I had everything a young boy could want. Each chapter of my life got me to a place no one could have seen coming—well, at least I couldn't have predicted it. From where I am today, writing this book, I can look back and see how each unique puzzle piece, each experience, each challenge and success, which may have seemed like they had no connection to each other, actually fit perfectly together.

Playing the Piano

My mother used to play the piano, and she encouraged her children to take lessons. I started taking lessons once a week. I did what many elementary school kids do when learning piano: practice only once a week for 10 minutes right before I had to leave for the lesson. This went on for years until I went to middle school.

I joined the chorus and discovered that the teacher needed someone to be the accompanist on the piano, so I volunteered. I remember the first song she asked me to learn, "Caberet."

With the music for Caberet in my hand, I didn't stop playing the piano from the minute I got home from school until bedtime. It became the sole focus of my life. My mother had to pull me away so I would go to bed. I had a purpose and a mission for practicing. When I started playing for the chorus, everybody knew I could play, and when someone needed an accompanist for the school talent show, most of the time, that was me. I loved playing and being on stage. Without me, the show could not go on, and it gave me a sense of purpose to be part of any musical production.

Piano became my life, and I continued to play in high school. I played for the chorus, stage musicals, soloists, talent shows, and concerts; I even played the xylophone in the marching band for a short time. My talent was blossoming. Besides playing the music of Billy Joel and Elton John, I started to play George Gershwin, Frédéric Chopin, and Sergei Rachmaninoff. My skills were expanding so fast that I thought about trying to get into the Harvard of music schools, the Julliard School of Music in New York City.

Like anything in life, if you are continually told you are great at something, you will likely be more passionate about it. Everyone marveled at my musical skills, and my head was filled with thoughts that I was the greatest piano player in the world.

My huge ego came tumbling down very quickly. Every two years, the county held a music festival for the high-school choruses. I attended the festival as a baritone singer, but what I *really* wanted was to be hanging out with the other pianists in attendance. I walked into a room with many pianos and what I saw and heard blew my mind. There were *so many* fantastic piano players!

They were playing things so beyond my capabilities. For example, I can read music but I can't play it by ear. I need written musical notes. Some of these students were playing songs they didn't know *without any music.* All they needed was someone to sing it for them. Then I saw them change the key of a song *on demand,* without having to figure out each note individually—a natural skill I didn't have. To ask me to switch the key of a song on demand would have been like asking me to dunk a basketball; it wasn't going to happen. What I was watching made it seem like I was already at Julliard. I had never seen pianists so talented except in the National Symphony.

My dreams were crushed. I still continued to play the piano, but my dreams of becoming a professional were gone. It wasn't until later in life that I learned a *very* important lesson: There is almost always someone better than you at what you do. If they aren't better than you, they eventually will be. This doesn't mean you have to be the best, you just need to be *good enough.* Being good enough will still allow you to succeed in any field.

Because the journey itself is the endgame, even if you don't go on to become great in something, you can still become highly successful in it and also learn some fantastic lessons.

Here are three suggestions to help you on your journey:

1. **Don't listen to negative thoughts or people.** When someone tells you that you can't do something, you could turn that into your reality. What is even more dangerous is *telling yourself* you can't do something. This is exactly what I did when I saw how fabulous the other piano players were. I took the idea of playing the piano professionally out of my future just by having negative thoughts.

2. **Understand the meaning of luck.** Luck is when preparation and opportunity meet. Technically, luck doesn't exist. You must be prepared for whatever you want to do in life and recognize when an opportunity presents itself. Many people want to win the lottery, but you can't win unless you play. You can't be a professional pianist without studying and

practicing piano for many years. You can't be successful in real-estate investing unless you learn the nuances of buying and selling real estate.

The most famous or successful person in any field is not always the best; they're the one who was prepared when an opportunity presented itself. Have you ever noticed that you don't have to be the best vocalist to be a successful singer? Just listen to Bob Dylan. There is a good argument to be made that opportunity can be more important than talent. This may be true in many areas of life. The success of many people involves having *just enough* talent, but more importantly, having an opportunity and taking advantage of it.

Most of us have been given tremendous talent to do *something.* We may not the best at it, but we are good enough that we could be successful if we stopped putting barriers in front of ourselves and kept moving forward. I could have been very successful playing the piano just by having had the right opportunity. Unfortunately, I never gave myself the chance to be a professional because I stopped believing it was possible. When an opportunity presents itself, people may sit around twiddling their thumbs and do nothing about it except make excuses or procrastinate. Then they wonder why they miss out on opportunities.

3. **Hang around with the right people.** We tend to be like the people with whom we spend time. If you hang around with people who don't want to be as awesome as possible or don't want to strive for greatness, you will most likely be the same way. This is why who your friends are is very important.

One of the biggest decisions you make when you get married and have children is where to live. It is always better to be around people who are positive and growth oriented.

It's the same way in sports. Playing with better athletes makes you better. I tell my son that I want him to find a chess player who will beat him consistently because if he's winning all the time, he may feel good about himself but it won't make him a better chess player.

If I had believed in myself more and had a few positive, growth-oriented people around me outside of the chorus department, maybe I would have kept my dream of professional piano playing alive. I'll never know if the right opportunity would have presented itself. Instead, what I did was *not* discover how awesome I could have become.

When I was single, I took my future wife to a musical in Washington, D.C. After the show, we walked through a hotel to get to the car. We happened to see a piano, and I nonchalantly sat down and played. As they say in sports, game over. I had her at middle C. For most of my life, any time I saw a piano, I would sit down and play it. I loved the attention and accolades. If you happened to have seen me in any hotel lobby, a Nordstrom's, or at a party, you would have heard me playing the piano. The attention I received is what compelled me to practice at great lengths to improve my ability. This played a major role later in my life.

My First Coin Adventure

One thing that propelled me forward in the coin business was the 1979 silver and gold boom. The price of silver increased from $6 to $50 an ounce.

Half dollars minted from 1964 and earlier, made with 90 percent silver, were out of circulation. Half dollars from 1965 through 1970 still contained 40 percent silver.

When silver had been $6 an ounce, it was not cost-effective to extract the silver from the 40-percent-silver half-dollars, so most of these were still circulating. When silver started trading at $50 an ounce, each 40-percent-silver half-dollar was now worth $3.

Many families were hunting for coins, so it was not that easy to walk into a bank and get half-dollar rolls. But my father had a great relationship with his banker, and one day he brought home hundreds of dollars' worth of half-dollar rolls.

My brother David and I found enough 40-percent-silver half-dollars in those rolls that when I sold them to a coin store, I made more than $50. That was a lot of money for a 14-year-old. I started to realize that there was a future for me in the coin business.

When I was 15, I was given a scholarship for a week-long coin seminar at Colorado College. That was an amazing learning experience because I'd thought I was the only young coin geek in the entire world. There were plenty of kids just like me at the seminar. The seminar was so good that the next year I went back, and I made friends who would help propel me into the coin business.

One of them was Dwight Manley. When Dwight finished high school, he did not attend college but went right into the coin business. I attended college and only dabbled in coins, but Dwight and I stayed in touch. He would encourage me to come to coin shows around the country. I almost dropped out of college after my second year to go into the coin business full time, but my parents wanted me to graduate, and I did not want to disappoint them.

Dwight went on to become an NBA sports agent, managing players like Karl Malone and Dennis Rodman. Dwight also went on to purchase one of the most expensive coin deals in the history of the world: the coins and gold bars from the shipwreck of the S.S. Central America. What an exciting journey he's had!

In March 1986, during my junior year in college, I had a burst of inspiration. I remember the exact moment when I made a decision that changed the trajectory of my life. Previously, during all my college breaks, I worked as a bank teller. It was easy: all I had to do was call the bank and they would ask me to show up for work. That's pretty sweet for a college student! But I decided that instead of working for the bank that summer, I would travel the country buying and selling coins. I made a conscious decision that I was not going to take the easy route.

In life, we have two choices: we can be comfortably mediocre or uncomfortably great. I turned down an easy job and a guaranteed paycheck for a challenging job with no guarantees of income. I was in charge of how and when I worked, where I went, and how I would go about buying and selling coins. I knew very few people in the business, but I knew *just enough* that I could get in the door. As some people would say, I knew enough to be dangerous.

I needed money to start my business, so I called Dwight. He told me to meet him at a coin show in Denver the following week. He had already been a very successful coin dealer for a number of years and had agreed to loan me money to start my business.

Before I left for Denver, I went to many of the local coin stores in the Maryland and Virginia area, acquiring inventory or getting coins on consignment. When I met Dwight at the show, he asked to see the coins I'd brought. He bought every single one of them, and I made $800 on that deal alone!

Looking back, I really had no idea what I was doing, but I knew *just enough*. Dwight loaned me $4,000. I paid him back (plus interest) six months later. I was now a coin dealer.

My Introduction to Teaching

After many successful decades of buying and selling coins, I was asked to teach at the same seminar I'd attended 35 years earlier. The class I taught was on United States coin grading. Coin grading is a talent needed for being a successful collector or dealer, and most people struggle to understand all the nuances that go into it.

Coin grading is about how coins are valued, just as diamond grading is about how diamonds are valued. You can have two diamonds that are each exactly one carat; they are the exact same weight and very close in size. One diamond is worth $1,000 and the other $20,000. Why the huge price difference? The variation is based on the carat weight, color, cut, and clarity of each stone. A grading expert can see all the nuances of each diamond and determine its value.

It's the same thing with coins, but with even larger variations in price. Anywhere there are variations in price, there is an opportunity to arbitrage off of minute differences. The larger the variations and the more of them, the more chances there are to find mispriced assets. This is how expert evaluators make money. It is very similar to what happens with real-estate investing. If you ask a real-estate investor how much a 1,000-square-foot condo is worth, they have no idea because dozens of variables determine the value. A condo on Madison Avenue in New York City may be worth $20 million while the same size in Laredo, Texas, is worth maybe $20,000 (sorry, Laredo).

While teaching at the coin seminar, I discovered that I had the ability to provide information in a way that people could clearly understand. What was even more important was that I *loved* teaching. I had never taught before and realized that it gave me a lot of energy. Any time I was able to teach a concept or idea that students understood, it gave me a boost of energy. I left the class every day completely exhausted because I had put so much of my heart and soul into teaching.

When you are teaching about how to grade coins, you're teaching others to see what you see. You have to be able to explain how your brain processes every nuance of every variable that goes into the grading process. As you will see later, this was a big piece of my life's puzzle.

In my grading seminar, one of the students, a teenager, became such a talented grader that he went on to become one of the most successful buyers of rare coins in the world. I seemed to have created some of my toughest competition, although he most likely would have been great without me.

In the coin business, I was considered to be at the top of my game. I had everything I'd ever dreamed of. *Do this, get that.* But I had this deep feeling that there had to be more to life, I just couldn't put my finger on it.

Every time my wife and I went to Florida for a vacation and to visit family, I saw a bunch of old men going out every morning to play golf. We spend most of our life working to be able to save up for retirement in order to do what? Wake up every morning and chase a little white ball around a golf course? That's how we're supposed to finish our puzzle? That's our endgame? I would think to myself that there had to be more to life.

Teaching about coins was just another piece of my puzzle, which I did not know would affect my choices in life many years later.

Learning about Spirituality

Around the time of my first child's birth, my wife was introduced to a woman named Lori Palatnik. She is an educator in the field of spirituality based on Jewish teachings. She has a way of teaching that is brilliant and inspiring. Very few people have her gift of communication. She could sell the Brooklyn Bridge to a potato farmer in the middle of Nebraska. She helped us on our paths to learn more about our purposes in life and living with more meaning.

We've occasionally gone to hear other fantastic speakers who covered content similar to hers. Every time I was inspired by a speaker, I thought to myself that this is what I would like to be doing in my life: inspiring others to reach their potential and get fired up and passionate about life! I wanted to be on that stage speaking just as I used to want to be on the stage playing piano.

I discovered a way that I could be on stage while helping other people. It seemed like a no-brainer that this is what I should be doing. Playing the piano was great and it made people feel good, but when I stopped playing, that feeling went away. I discovered an opportunity to teach something that would make people feel great about themselves and help them improve their lives. And unlike with the piano, people would *continue* to feel good about themselves long after they heard me speak.

Besides, the wisdom that I was learning was so deep and eye-opening that I knew that if I were to ever be in a position to teach, I would get tremendous amounts of energy from it, just as I had when I was teaching coin grading. I knew that if I had a decent audience, my energy level would be so high that I would be able to motivate people to make changes that would better their lives.

Helping other people had never been the focus of my life. My focus was on how I was going to find my next big coin deal. When I was able to make a big profit on a deal, what should I do with the money? Where should I go or what should I buy? My life was *Do this, get that* because that's all I knew. I was trained from a young age to try to upgrade my possessions; I fell into the trap of materialism.

Unless you're raised in a spiritual home with spiritual values, upgrading possessions can easily become the purpose of your life. Helping people and being a giver is not necessarily on your radar as being the ultimate in fulfilling your purpose in life.

Lori taught my wife and me that there is a lot more to life. There is nothing wrong with wearing a Rolex watch and driving a Ferrari. But if your life focus is on what you own, you may be one of many people who are now unhappy, divorced, or on antidepressants. Lori triggered something inside me that got me thinking more deeply about life. Becoming a retired old man traipsing to the golf course was not something that would fulfill me. Helping others in whatever ways I could seemed to make more sense than trying to hit a little white ball into a small hole in as few shots as possible.

The Puzzle Started to Take Shape

I loved playing piano, being on stage, and being the center of attention. What I loved even more was how I made people feel. That fed my passion for playing piano. Anyone who watched me play walked away feeling better, and the ability to make people feel good was a contributing factor that made me want to teach.

While teaching coin collectors how to grade, I learned to present information in a way that people could easily understand. The material I had to share was difficult to teach because I had to get others to see things that I could see. When you love something, as I did coins, you put your heart and soul into it and you can likely be pretty good at teaching it.

I had the two ingredients that were the driving force for me to want to teach: the desire to be on stage and the skill of and passion for teaching. Even though I didn't realize that the thought of teaching was lurking in the back of my mind, the right opportunity presented itself and I jumped on it. I loved to make people feel good because it made me feel good, and teaching fulfilled this desire.

Then I learned about spirituality and how every person can make a difference. You don't have to come from a rich or famous family to make an impact in the world. Every person has the ability to change the world for the better, as long as they don't make excuses or waste their time on meaningless endeavors.

When I started listening to great speakers, I decided that speaking was what I wanted to do. I didn't want to *Do this, get that.* I wanted to *Do this, live that!* I saw other people making a difference in the lives of their students, and I wanted to be helping others and changing lives.

I even felt like I had a way to reach more people than some of the speakers I heard. Sometimes writers and speakers can be too smart for the average person. I thought that many of them were almost *too* brilliant. I would hear speakers and read books, and some of the content would go over my head. There is a skill to presenting information in a way that the average person can understand, and I thought I had that ability.

The Big C: The Trigger That Started It All

I used to play basketball every Sunday afternoon. We played outside during the hot and humid Washington, D.C., summers. It was usually a full-court game that lasted two hours. It was a lot of fun, but every Monday, my back would be *killing* me. It hurt so much that I had to get out of my car by grabbing the top of the open driver side door and pulling myself out. My wife noticed this and said I should go see a chiropractor. I refused. I'm a guy; I don't need to see a doctor.

I knew the cause of the pain was from playing basketball. My wife and I went back and forth for months about the chiropractor until one day she said, "If you go to the chiropractor, it will be my birthday *and* anniversary present. I'll even make the appointment and it will be across the street from your office." So I said "Twist my arm" and agreed to go.

The chiropractor took an X-ray of my back. She asked if anyone had seen an X-ray of my lungs recently, and I told her no. She showed me on the X-ray that there was a shadow in my lung that was not supposed to be there. As soon as I left her office, I called Virtual Physical because I'd heard their advertisements on the radio. They specialize in CT scans of your body and review the results with you.

The next day, I had the scan. The radiologist said there was a 1.8-centimeter mass in my right lung. I asked what that was. He would not give me an answer and told me to see a pulmonologist.

The next day, I walked into a pulmonologist's office and handed him my scan. He said, "Let's take your lung out." I said, "What? You want to take my lung out? I'm only 47, I run 3 miles a day, I don't smoke, I don't do drugs, I don't eat meat, I don't drink...before 3 p.m."

A few months later, I had the upper lobe of my lung removed, and the results from the biopsy showed that it was cancer.

When I was in recovery, Lori came to visit me. She said something that changed the trajectory of my life. She said "This will make a great class someday."

And that is exactly what I did: I created a class called "Acquiring Greatness." I used the acronym GREAT and used the challenge of overcoming cancer as the back story. I then developed many other classes using stories from my life. Everything that ever happened to me was part of my journey, even the cancer.

That is how I started writing books. When you develop and teach classes, they can take on lives of their own, and one class can morph into a new concept. This is why one of the secrets in this book is "Always Be Moving Forward." It can take you to places you never thought possible. This is true in many aspects of life, including the spiritual and financial realms. I certainly had plenty of stories to tell from my life, which, at a minimum, made the experience interesting if not inspirational.

How the Food Network Changed My Life

Once when I was at a hotel in Fort Lauderdale, Florida, for a coin convention, I happened to turn on the TV to the Food Network. I watched a show called *Chopped* and it blew me away. Not because the show was that fantastic but because it had a lesson that was perfect for marriages. I was discovering that almost anything can be the basis for a class. There are lessons to be learned from almost all mundane daily activities. The show became the basis for my first relationship class. I called it "Chopped: Get Your Marriage Cooking." It was my favorite class to teach (probably because it had to do with food).

When my family moved to Israel, I started to teach for a program in the Old City of Jerusalem. Some of the other educators who speak there are people who inspired me 10 years earlier. Some of the classes are on history, spiritual motivation, and finding your purpose.

I starting teaching there in summer 2019 and was having an amazing time. The best way I can describe the experience of teaching is like being a budding basketball star who grows up and gets to play in the NBA with Michael Jordan: starstruck and playing with one's mentors. I was speaking in the same program with speakers who had inspired me for years.

I was teaching students who *loved* what I was teaching them. They wanted to be there and learn as much from me as possible. People who enjoyed my classes were growth oriented and open to learning.

I noticed that my students were more willing to learn in Israel than the people I'd taught back in the Washington, D.C., area. I viewed this phenomenon as like having a cactus sitting on the windowsill in the kitchen: it stays small its entire life. But if you go to the desert in Arizona, you see *huge* cacti. Why? A windowsill isn't the best environment for a cactus to reach its potential. You have to be in the right environment and around the right people to grow. Living in Washington, with its focus on work and politics, is not the best place for someone to ignite their soul.

When we arrived in Israel, I was very excited to introduce my Chopped class to a new audience. I noticed that I was not getting as many students as I was for my other classes. So I decided to change the name of the class to "The Ten Secrets" and develop separate versions for dating and marriage. The name change worked and my class sizes increased significantly. My dating classes became standing-room only, and I kept getting requests to post the content online.

That's when I decided to write a book based on these topics.

My first book, *The Ten Secrets to Find the Love of Your Life,* took me only a few weeks to write. My second, *The Ten Secrets to A Passionate Marriage,* took about a month. I had most of the material in my head, so I was able to get these books written and published very quickly.

If you had asked me 10 years ago if I would ever write a book, I would have said no and asked if you were crazy. If you had asked any of my friends from college, they would have said the same thing. I was the guy who organized keg parties, not the one who was going to be an author.

When I look back, I can see how every single thing that has happened to me—whether it was a challenge, opportunity, failure, or success—has helped me get to where I am in life.

Think about all the puzzle pieces *you* have put together. Some of them may not have fit together easily, but when you look back, you can see how the difficult pieces made your puzzle beautifully intricate. Who wants a boring life with puzzle pieces that fit together without any effort? It's the challenges that make the puzzle unique.

Life is amazing, and even more so when you look back and see how everything that's happened to you has been part of your journey to where you are now. Who would have thought cancer would have propelled me into teaching and eventually writing?

Look at all of your challenges and see how they have made you the person you are.

When I was in college, taking the job at the bank would have been easy and comfortable. Making the decision to choose the uncomfortable route, to take a risk and go work in the coin business, on my own with no experience, helped me become not just a success but somewhat of a sensation.

You can go through life and be comfortably mediocre, or you can embrace something uncomfortable and increase your chances of achieving greatness.

You must decide how much you're willing to grow and break down the barriers that are keeping you from being awesome. When you figure out what you can do to make a difference in the world and then go achieve it, one day, you will look back and realize that you've made a great impact.

What started out in 7th grade as my wanting to play piano for the junior-high-school chorus has turned into your reading a book about how to discover how awesome you really are. You never know where life is going to lead. Every step along the way is your journey, and when you figure out that the journey *is* the endgame, you will enjoy it so much more.

Your endgame isn't *Do this, get that,* then chase a little white ball around. It's *Do this, live that!* When you can start living your life and enjoying the journey, you'll find out that you're awesome.

Acknowledgments

A tremendous thank you to my wife, Ilana, and our family, for allowing me to take the time to write. I am blessed to have you all in my life.

A big thank you to all my music teachers, especially Mrs. Golding and Mr. Aiken, who trusted me to accompany their choruses on the piano.

Thank you to all the vocal soloists in high school for letting me play for you. You really helped me on my journey and those wonderful memories will always be with me.

Thank you to all the rabbis and their wives who guided me toward having clarity about life and showed me what real gratitude means.

Finally, a big thank you to the Creator for blessing me with so many gifts.

About the Author

Daniel lives in Jerusalem with his wife, five children, and a Labradoodle. He started his career as a coin dealer and now spends his time writing and teaching. You can contact Daniel at FindYourAwesomebook@ gmail.com.

Made in the USA
Monee, IL
10 June 2021

70702101R00108